Creating
Short Fiction

Also by Damon Knight

NOVELS

A for Anything
Beyond the Barrier
CV
Double Meaning
The Earth Quarter
Hell's Pavement
Humpty Dumpty

The Man in the Tree
Natural State
The Observers
The Other Foot
A Reasonable World
Why Do Birds
The World and Thorinn

COLLECTIONS

The Best of Damon Knight
Better Than One (with Kate
  Wilhelm)
Far Out
God's Nose
In Deep

Late Knight Edition
Off Center
One Side Laughing
Rule Golden & Other Stories
Turning On
World Without Children and the
  Earth Quarter

NONFICTION

Charles Fort: Prophet of the
  Unexplained

The Futurians
In Search of Wonder

TRANSLATIONS

Ashes, Ashes by René Barjavel

13 French Science Fiction Stories

AS EDITOR

Best Stories from Orbit
Beyond Tomorrow
A Century of Great Short
  Science Fiction Novels
A Century of Science Fiction
Cities of Wonder
The Dark Side
Dimension X
First Contact
First Voyages (with Martin H.
  Greenberg)
The Golden Road
Happy Endings
100 Years of Science Fiction
The Metal Smile
Monad, 1–3

Nebula Award Stories One
Now Begins Tomorrow
Orbit, vols. 1–21
Perchance to Dream
A Pocketful of Stars
A Science Fiction Argosy
Science Fiction Inventions
Science Fiction of the Thirties
The Shape of Things
A Shocking Thing
Tomorrow and Tomorrow
Tomorrow x 4
Toward Infinity
Turning Points
Westerns of the Forties
Worlds to Come

Creating
Short Fiction

THIRD EDITION

DAMON KNIGHT

ST. MARTIN'S GRIFFIN
NEW YORK

Grateful acknowledgment is made for permission to reprint excerpts from the following:

Cerf, Bennett. *Try and Stop Me,* copyright 1971 by Mrs. Bennett Cerf, Christopher Cerf, and Jonathan Cerf. Reprinted by permission of Simon & Schuster.
Fouhy, Joan. Item in "Life in These United States," December 1978, *Reader's Digest.* Reprinted by permission of *Reader's Digest.*
Hammett, Dashiell. *The Maltese Falcon,* copyright 1929, 1930 by Alfred A. Knopf and renewed 1957, 1958 by Dashiell Hammett. Reprinted by permission of Alfred A. Knopf, Inc.
Hawthorne, Nathaniel. *The American Notebooks.* Edited by Claude M. Simpson. Volume VIII of the Centenary Edition of the Works of Nathaniel Hawthorne (Columbus: Ohio State University Press, 1972), p. 97.
Hemingway, Ernest. *Death in the Afternoon,* copyright 1932 by Charles Scribner's Sons, renewal copyright 1960 by Ernest Hemingway. Reprinted by permission of Charles Scribner's Sons.
Lagerlof, Selma. "A Christmas Guest." Reprinted by permission of Doubleday and Company, Inc.
O'Hara, John. "I Spend My Days in Longing" from *The Horse Knows the Way,* copyright 1964 by John O'Hara. Reprinted by permission of Random House, Inc.
Poe, Edgar Allan. "The Cask of Amontillado." Reprinted by permission of Doubleday and Company, Inc.
Twain, Mark. "How I Edited an Agricultural Paper" from *Sketches New and Old.* Harper & Row, Publishers, Inc.

Library of Congress Cataloging-in-Publication Data

Knight, Damon Francis.
   Creating short fiction / Damon Knight.—[Rev., updated ed.]
     p. cm.
   Includes bibliographical references (p. 199) and index.
   ISBN 0-312-15094-6
   1. Fiction—Authorship. 2. Short story. I. Title.
PN3373.K6 1997
808.3´1—dc20   96-34412
                                    CIP

First published in the United States of America by Writer's Digest Books

20 19 18 17 16 15 14 13 12 11

CONTENTS

Part 3

Beginning a Story

Part 4

Controlling a Story

Part 5   Finishing a Story

Part 6

Being a Writer

LIST OF EXERCISES

To Robin Scott Wilson,
who unlocked the door, and
To Carol Cartaino
and Howard I. Wells III,
who opened it wide

Tender of lip and nostril,
Rose-fingered, sturdy of limb
(Mine the watering, mine
The manure of old hopes),
How they strain to be free!
See the young roots rise
Dripping earth to earth,
Stem, flower and shoot
Gleaming like otters
As they run to the dawn.
And I, crisp as an old leaf,
Feel the green veins stir.

Three Reasons Why I Should Not Have Written This Book:

1. Writing can only be learned, not taught.

2. Even if it can be taught, you can't learn to write by reading a book.

3. Even if you can learn that way, you may stifle your creativity by learning too much about processes that should be spontaneous and automatic.

These three statements contradict each other, and yet I think they are all partly true. It's true that you must write if you want to learn to write. It's true that you can't build a good story like a piece of mail-order furniture, just by following the directions on the box. And it's also true that the unconscious works better if you don't watch it too closely.

Years ago, if you had suggested to me that writing couldn't be taught, I would probably have agreed, partly out of indifference—I didn't care if it could be taught or not—and partly because, like the other professional writers I knew, I had learned to write without any formal instruction. I didn't know how or why I was doing what I did, and I couldn't have told anybody else how to do it.

Later I worked in a reading-fee agency in New York, where I wrote letters to clients explaining that their stories were no good because they did not follow the "plot skeleton." I believed this, too, at the time; I believed in the plot skeleton and the villain and the hero and all that, but only for others, not for myself—I believed I had found a unique and underhanded way of working outside the rules that everyone else had to follow.

Still later, in writing workshops, I found myself trying to teach the few things I had learned about writing, and in the process discovering that some of them were not true. (It is not true, for instance, that every story has to have a plot skeleton; it is not even true that every story has to have a *plot*.)

When my wife and I began teaching at the Clarion Workshop in 1968, we were both veterans of the Milford Writers' Conference, but neither of us had ever taught beginners. We learned that the first thing we had to do, and by far the hardest, was to find out what the students didn't know. We discovered, for instance, that many young writers had never heard of viewpoint; others didn't know what a plot was. (One student told us, "I thought a story was just a bunch of interesting things happening.") The next step was to analyze viewpoint, or plot, or whatever—something we had never had to do before. Only then could we devise some way of teaching it—usually an exercise. This process has continued year after year at the Clarion Workshop, now a summer program at Michigan State University; there is always something else some student doesn't know.

Assuming that the techniques of writing can be taught, as I now believe, *should* they be taught? I don't think this is a frivolous question. I have known writers who were afraid they wouldn't be able to write anymore, or wouldn't want to, if they found out too much about their own creative processes. I can't dismiss the possibility that some reader of this book, by prodding her unconscious, might make it close up like an anemone. So why take a chance? After all, people got along without writing manuals for thousands of years, just as they got along without sex manuals.

I suppose the reason is that in spite of many disappointments I still believe that the pursuit of knowledge is good. Even if I thought writing was an antisocial activity (and sometimes I do), I would still try to find out things nobody else knows, and I would still try to tell you.

This book, like all books, is a message in a bottle. I know who I am, but I can only guess who you are—the persons who open the bottle, read the message. When I think about you, I see faces in a classroom, because that's where I usually encounter beginning writers. You are a bright-eyed bunch, healthy-looking and alert, but there is nothing about any one of you that says unmistakably, "I am a writer."

Creativity is a word I don't like to use, because I don't know what it means, and because it drops so easily from the tongues of educators and psychologists who don't know what it means either. (The psychologists have been trying to measure it for years, without any luck, because they have no idea what they're measuring.) Nevertheless, I understand the desire to make something that has never existed before. If you feel this urge too, we can talk about it without having to know what it is or where it comes from.

Psychologists have found out a little bit about the personalities of writers. They are individualists, skeptics, taboo-breakers, mockers, loners; they are undependable, likely to be behind on their rent; they keep irregular hours and have strange friends. Professional writers, like criminals, really live outside society: they have no regular jobs, they come and go as they please, they live by their wits.

Writers in my experience are more inquisitive about a broader range of things than most people; they are more intelligent, more interesting to talk to, and more unconventional in their attitudes. Writers are people who don't like to work for other people. They have vivid fantasy lives, and they feel a need to express their inner experiences in a form that can be seen, heard, or touched.

You may know all these things about yourself and still be wondering if you can have a career as a writer. That depends, not just on talent or aptitude, but on determination and luck.

Writing talent is probably more common than anybody suspects, and it is less important to a writer's career than most people believe. I have known highly talented young people who for one reason or another have dropped out of writing and never reappeared, and I've known people with very modest talents who by sheer determined effort have become professionals. I can't pump determination into you, and wouldn't if I could. What I can do is try to tell you what you're in for, and help you acquire the skills that make the difference between the amateur writer and the professional.

A successful story, like a healthy organism, is all one thing, not just a collection of parts. Everything in it fits together, flows together, harmonizes. If every story were successful, there would be no reason other than academic curiosity to talk about the component parts of stories. It's when something goes wrong, or when you're trying to master a new skill, that you need to know what the components are and how they work.

Many of my old friends take the view that because they taught themselves, others should be able to do the same. They forget the gray years when they were struggling toward their eventual "instinctive" understanding of how to write. Writing is like riding a bicycle; once you can do it, it seems the most natural thing in the world. But how many times did you have to fall off before you learned?

Large parts of this book have a dogmatic tone, which is really more honest than the cultivated humility of this introduction. By nature I am egotistical, opinionated, and self-centered, and the only thing that keeps me from displaying these qualities more than I do is the example of certain colleagues whose public self-admiration makes me giggle. If I could suppress my dogmatic tendencies entirely, I would; perhaps I will be able to by the time I am eighty, but in the meantime I want to warn you to distrust all ex-cathedra statements about writing, including mine. Don't imagine that you are necessarily wrong if every authority disagrees with you. Your problems are unique, like everybody else's problems, and you will find your own solutions or perish. What would be the point of my telling you that you should have found some other solution?

Finally, in spite of everything I say here, you may be tempted to think that all you have to do is follow my directions, fitting part A to part B, in order to construct a story. I don't say this because I think you are dumb; Richard McKenna, one of the brightest, wisest, and most talented writers I ever knew, made a similar mistake and wrote about it in an essay called "Journey with a Little Man," the best piece of writing about writing I know of.

Try to improve your writing one piece at a time—work on your characterization, for instance, or dialogue, or plotting, until you have made some progress; then turn to another aspect and work on that. If you try to learn everything all at once, you will paralyze yourself (like the caterpillar who was asked in what order he moved his legs), by too much *conscious* attention to the rules.

As you use this book (here I assume that this copy belongs to you), I would like you to try an experiment. Mark the passages that seem especially useful now with a colored pen. Later, when you have made some progress as a writer, go through the book again and this time mark relevant and useful passages in a different color. Later on, use a third color. Eventually the book may look like a rainbow; I hope so.

I can't remember all the people who have helped me, but I want to thank my colleagues at the Milford Conference, with whom I debated acrimoniously for twenty years, and my students and fellow teachers in the Clarion Workshop at Michigan State University. I am deeply indebted to my wife, Kate Wilhelm, who has taught with me at Clarion from the beginning, and from whom I learned many of the insights and techniques set forth here.

Damon Knight

Note: The sections of this book and the exercises that go with them are arranged in a linear order. I can't help that—there are no nonlinear books—but I want to remind you that the topics dealt with here are all interrelated. You may find it convenient to do the exercises in the order in which they are given, or in some other order: it doesn't matter. My advice would be to do the most challenging ones first, but please don't neglect the others—some of them are not as simple as they look.

Part 1

Developing Your Talent As a Writer

"You Are Extraordinary"

In a remarkable book called *You Are Extraordinary,* Roger J. Williams wrote that if there were as much variation in the visible parts of our anatomy as there is in our internal arrangements, some of us would have noses the size of navy beans and some the size of watermelons. Charts in his book show the "textbook stomach" and then a dozen or so real stomachs, all different; the "textbook liver" and then a page of real livers. Even the number of muscles and the way they are attached is variable. Veins and arteries, tendons, blood cells, ductless glands are all organized differently in every human being.

In the brain, too, there is enormous variability. The kinds and numbers of cells in a given area are different inside every skull. Your brain is more individual than your fingerprints.

Among the writers I have known, one habitually worked lying down in the dark, in a trailer with its windows painted black, dictating into a tape recorder. Another, when he wanted to think about a new novel, got on a bus to a destination about four hours away—it didn't matter where. When he arrived, he boarded another bus and rode back; by the time he got home, he would have the novel all plotted out. Another meditated about a novel for three months, then sat down in a specially designed cubicle, smaller than a telephone booth, and typed furiously for thirty hours straight. When he came out, the novel was done.

It follows that you must learn to write your own way, or you can never learn at all. I don't mean that you can do whatever you please; you still have to communicate with the rest of us. I just mean that nobody can tell you exactly how to do it. "Here are the rules," I say; but when you are skilled enough, you will certainly bend some of these rules and break others.

"Writing talent" is not all one thing: it is a cluster of abilities—

verbal facility, imagination, "storytelling ability," sense of drama, of structure, of rhythm, and probably a lot of others that nobody has put a name to. You may have a great ear for dialogue, for instance, but be poor at visual description; or you may be weak at plotting but have a strong narrative sense. Your first job is to find out your strengths and weaknesses—many of the exercises in this book are designed to help you do so—and your second is to learn to get the most out of what you have.

Later we will be discussing the various skills that a writer needs, but first I want to tell you about the four stages that nearly every writer has to pass through.

Four Stages of a Writer's Development

Stage 1. You are writing for yourself, and your stories are essentially daydreams. They please you in a sort of narcissistic way, but they are not stories that communicate to other people. (I'm not against narcissism in moderation; I believe that you have to love yourself before you can love anyone else. All I'm saying is that if you want to be a writer, narcissistic fantasy isn't enough.)

Stage 2. Now you are trying to break out of the shell, trying to communicate, but your stories are what editors call "trivial." You are not ready yet to write a completely developed story, and you're trying to get away with half-formed ones. The rejection slips tell you that you're not succeeding.

Stage 3. You are writing complete stories, or reasonable imitations, but you are being held back by technical problems, usually weaknesses in structure or character.

Stage 4. You have solved these problems, at least well enough to get by, and now you are working at a professional level. (There are stages beyond 4, but after that the author no longer needs help.)

People who start writing late in life often seem to skip stage 1 and sometimes stage 2 as well. I would almost be tempted to recommend that you leave writing alone until you are in your early thirties, but what if writing is all you want to do? You're going to have to go the route, frustrations and all, just as I did.

It took me about twelve years to work my way into stage 4. It may take you more or less time to travel the same distance, depending on your age, experience, talent, determination, and luck.

I think what happens when we are learning to write is that we keep weaving baskets of words that are too large or small, too strong or weak. In the beginning our baskets are very small and we don't try to put much in them. Then the baskets get stronger and bigger, too big for what's inside, and they collapse into awkward shapes. And then we begin putting more into the baskets, but now it is too much, and the baskets break: and so on, until at last we reach some accommodation between the basket and its contents. By now we have forgotten the seesaw process that brought us to this point, but we use it instinctively, like any artist—balancing strength against weight, weaving baskets of words just the right size for what they have to contain.

When I was about fifteen I began a story in which a young man invented a matter duplicator and copied himself several times. I wrote the first scene, in which the five identical heroes were standing around saying, in effect, "Well, here we are." I had a notion that I would put them into a spaceship and send them off to have adventures, but nothing came to mind and the story never got any further. This was pure stage 1—a narcissistic daydream. (I was an only child, and I wanted somebody to talk to.)

A year or so later, after many failures, I managed to finish a story. It was two pages long, single-spaced, typed on both sides of the paper. The story was about a dying Martian race that encoded the minds of some of its members in a computerlike device and left the device in a highly visible monument. The monument was a trap: if space travelers ever came to the planet, they would investigate the monument, whereupon the device would impress the dead Martians' minds on their brains, and the Martians, in effect, would live again. At the end of the story I revealed that the Martians were six-legged, whereas the Earthmen who discovered the monument had only four limbs. Therefore the Martians couldn't control their bodies, and the transformed Earthmen lay there and died. I thought this ending was profoundly ironic. What it was, was too simple and arbitrary—"trivial." The characters were not people but interchangeable parts; the story had no development, no complication, just a beginning and an end without any middle section. It was a stage 2 story.

I wrote other stories of this kind and sold some of them when I was nineteen or twenty. One, written during World War II, was called "Blackout." In this one the stars turned out to be street lights in a metagalactic city under attack by a supercosmic enemy. I'm sure you can guess the ending. The story was a crude attempt at something Arthur C. Clarke later did superbly in "The Nine Billion Names of God."

When I was nineteen, I wrote a story about a group of explorers who had themselves reduced to microscopic size and got into various kinds of trouble. The story was written in the form of a message from the explorers appealing for help to the scientist who had shrunk them. It was never published, and no wonder; the plot was episodic and unoriginal. Nevertheless, it was a breakthrough for me—it was a story of normal length rather than a short-short—a stage 3 story.

What was happening to me here was something that I see happening to a lot of young writers in this stage. They are trying to create plots of some complexity, and they find this so difficult that they skimp on the characters. As a result, even when the plot is well constructed (and it seldom is), the story is unsuccessful because the characters are puppets and no one cares what becomes of them.

The first story I wrote that I would claim as stage 4 was "Not with a Bang," published in 1950. It had a trick-ending plot, but succeeded in being nontrivial because I knew my characters and loved them. In this one, humanity had been wiped out by a nuclear war except for one man and one woman, who met in a restaurant in Salt Lake City. The man was a nasty little cripple, suffering from a disease that in its final stage would cause recurrent episodes of total paralysis. He had medication for it, but when he was paralyzed he wouldn't be able to give it to himself. The woman was a dotty ex-nurse who had regressed to her Methodist childhood, and who resisted the man's advances because no minister was alive to marry them.* At length he persuaded her, only to be struck down by paralysis when he went to the men's room. She would never open that door, of course.

Getting Out of Stage 1

If you are in the daydreaming stage and would like to get out of it, do this: Take all the principal parts in your daydream, not just the central one. At first it may be like playing chess against yourself (not very satisfactory, especially if you cheat), but in time you will learn the pleasure of letting every character act for himself. Suppose, for example, that in your daydream it has just been discovered that you are the missing heir to the throne of a small Balkan kingdom. Clad in scarlet and ermine, you are surrounded by murmuring courtiers who marvel at your youth and beauty. Now select one of these courtiers and play his part for a while. Look at yourself through his eyes—how does he *really* see this gawky upstart from another country? Ouch! There goes the sweet golden daydream, but you may have the beginnings of a story.

Writing attracts some people as a way of concealing themselves, hiding inside imaginary characters, in the same way that an actor can hide inside the role he is playing. Certainly concealment is part of writing, and we all hide in our characters; but writing is also a way of revealing ourselves. Either we do this voluntarily and courageously, or we do it out of timidity and in spite of ourselves. The unhappy young writer who invents heroes of stupefying intelligence, wisdom, beauty, strength, and virtue is like a child trying to hide behind a fencepost. She can't hide all of herself, or even choose which parts to reveal.

---

*Years later, when I was editing a series of anthologies, I got a manuscript from an unknown writer in which *both* the survivors felt this way. At the end of the story they agreed to set out on a journey around the world, because there must be a Baptist minister alive somewhere. And the author, who from the style of his misspellings was obviously Southern, ended with the line: "That makes since."

All these narcissistic daydreams are designed to soothe and flatter one person—you. If you allowed any other character to follow his own interests, be a person in his own right, you would destroy the dream; that's why I want you to do it.

In a daydream, the game is rigged in favor of the central character, because that character is you. That's all right for a daydream, but there is no tension in a *story* in which the game is rigged in favor of the hero. Please take my word for it; once you have learned to play the storytelling game fairly, it will be much more exciting and satisfactory than your daydreams ever were.

Getting out of stage 2 and stage 3 is a matter of technique, with which the rest of this book deals; but technique won't help you much until you are out of stage 1.

Learning to See

You may think this section is superfluous; if you have normal vision, of course you imagine that you know how to see. Nevertheless, painters, sculptors, photographers, and writers, too, have to learn to see all over again in a different way. "To see" doesn't mean just to register images; it means to *interpret*. A camera doesn't see. A human being with his frontal lobes surgically removed could do what a camera does, if his visual system were intact, but he wouldn't *see*, because there would be nobody home. (Without a receiver, there is no signal.)

In *Death in the Afternoon*, Ernest Hemingway wrote about a bullfighter who was gored in the thigh: "As he stood up I saw the heavy, soiled gray silk of his rented trousers open cleanly and deeply to show the thigh bone from the hip almost to the knee. He saw it too and looked very surprised and put his hand on it while people jumped over the barrier and ran toward him to carry him to the infirmary."

Hemingway's bullfighter friends had no sympathy for this man, because he had done something unprofessional and stupid and had asked for what he got. "For myself," Hemingway wrote, "not being a bullfighter, and being much interested in suicides, the problem was one of depiction and waking in the night I tried to remember what it was that seemed just out of my remembering and that was the thing that I had really seen and, finally, remembering all around it, I got it. When he stood up, his face white and dirty and the silk of his breeches opened from waist to knee, it was the dirtiness of the rented breeches, the dirtiness of his slit underwear and the clean, clean, unbearably clean whiteness of the thigh bone that I had seen, and it was that which was important."

Notice that it isn't the description that matters, it's the meaning. "Meaning," "information," and "beauty" are all pretty much the same thing. Take any work of art, cut it into small pieces and re-arrange them at random. The result will be a meaningless jumble of words or shapes, uninformative and ugly.

I studied art for a year after high school, and I still see as an artist does. A tree to me is architecture of a peculiarly complex and sat-isfying kind, and it is also a complex and elegant pattern of color. Botanists and plant physiologists probably see a tree in a quite dif-ferent but equally interesting way. Maybe a log scaler looks at a tree in her neighbor's yard and sees how many board feet she could get out of it; a cabinetmaker or a woodcarver sees how the grain will look when it is sanded, stained, and varnished. When I was a child, I didn't see any of this—just "a tree," undifferentiated and unin-teresting (unless it had branches that I wanted to climb or fruit that I wanted to eat).

Outside the glass doors of my kitchen there is a lilac bush where various small birds alight on their way to the bird feeder, and re-cently I have found myself looking at that bush every morning for an hour or so. The branches and leaves with their delicate colors are like a stained glass window; the patterns are so complex that I never get tired of them. (I found out years ago that I did not dare have my desk beside a window with a tree outside it.) When I think about drawing the lilac bush, I realize how much order there is in all that complexity. The stems tilt away from the center, the outer ones just enough more than the inner ones to give every stem space for its branches and twigs. The angles at which the branches leave the stems are precisely determined—wider for the lower branches, narrower for the upper ones. The tips of the branches stop when they reach an invisible boundary, all but one or two mavericks. The bush looks exuberant, unrestrained, but in fact it is intensely lawful.

I'm not sure I had any perception of that kind when I was an art student—I think I just wanted to learn how to draw, and I realized that I had to understand how things were related in order to draw them accurately. But now it seems to me that the more you train your mind to perceive order, the more joy you are likely to get from the perception. Discoveries about natural law, the orderly relationships of parts to a whole, are deeply satisfying, not only to scientists but to painters, sculptors, musicians, and writers.

If you have ever had one of these sudden apprehensions of orderliness in the universe you will know what I mean. It's like a jolt of energy; you feel as if your eyes were lighting up and your hair standing on end. (Psychologists call it the "Aha!" reaction.)

I think this sensation is pleasurable to us for the same reason that sex is, because people who feel that kind of pleasure are likelier to survive, and have offspring who survive, than those who don't. This joy in discovery, or even the simple satisfaction of curiosity, is built into us, and probably it is built into all complex organisms. There is a cat in my family who is intensely curious about the connectivity of our house; he can't rest until he goes through any door he hasn't been through before. This kind of inquisitiveness has survival value—for us, anyhow; I'm not sure about cats—because anything we discover may be important, if not to us as individuals, then to our group and our descendants.

A short story, unlike other forms of representational art, must have people in the foreground; there is no fictional equivalent of landscape or still life. ("People" are not always human beings; they may be rabbits, as in *Watership Down,* or aliens from another planet, or personified elements of nature, as in George R. Stewart's *Fire* and *Storm.*) But you can't make sense of people in isolation, and so all the other things that science and art deal with come into writing too.

Curiously enough, the formal study of psychology is of less use to a writer than most other studies. Since we ourselves are the objects of investigation, common sense and common knowledge overlap formal psychology almost completely; the behavioral psychologists have taught us something about rats, but not much about people. (The psychologists would probably reply that they are not allowed to experiment on people.) Depth psychology, the psychology of Freud, Jung, and Adler, is an exception to this because it deals with the parts of our psyches that are unconscious.

With this qualification, I want to say that any system that helps you understand the world around you is valuable to you as a writer: natural history, biology, ethnology, physics, geology. . . . You must have knowledge to make the nets in which other knowledge is caught.

I don't mean to suggest that you ought to become a specialist in any field; on the contrary, I think you ought to be a generalist— you ought to have a scattered general knowledge of all kinds of things, in order to be able to see the broad relationships that are often invisible to a specialist. For the same reason, you need not become an authority on the short story, or on the English novel, but you should read widely in fiction. Some of my students in recent years have told me that they read very little fiction—they watch television and movies. I find this appalling. Would you try to become a doctor without studying medicine, or an actor without studying plays, or even going to the theater?

Not long ago a former student sent me a story that prompted me to ask him what authors, if any, he had taken as models for the kind of thing he was writing. The story was full of Victorian clichés, and I'm sure he didn't know it, because he had never read the Victorians.

You must be free to make your own mistakes and your own discoveries; I believe that, but I also believe that nothing exists in isolation. The lilac bush and the spread fingers of my hand and the branches of a coral are related, and so are the stories of John Cheever and Flannery O'Connor and Leo Tolstoy and Alice Munro. Here you swing, a leaf on a twig on a branch in the wind, and you tell me there is no tree?

Two Exercises in Seeing

1. Go and look at some living thing—a bush, a sleeping dog, a spider in her web—and keep looking until you feel you know something about it that you didn't know before. (If the thing you pick turns out not to be saying anything to you, try another one.) Now write a paragraph about it, trying to express that understanding in words. When you are done, you may have transformed your own image of the thing you looked at; it will never again be as uninteresting as it was before.

2. A game that I sometimes play on buses is to examine a couple of people sitting near me and make mental notes of their general appearance, their clothing, any peculiarities, etc. I find that I remember these people much more clearly than other people on the same bus, and that if I later write down a description of the people, I remember it still better.

Try this next time you are in a public place. Airports are good, waiting rooms of all kinds, concerts, malls—anyplace where you can watch people without calling attention to yourself.

Choose a person whose appearance interests you, and try to describe him in particular rather than in general. You are writing a sketch, not a police report; don't write "White male, 35–40, appr. 150 lbs., 5´10˝, wearing blue denim jacket, blue slacks, loafers." That is a general description that would enable the police to scoop up five or six hundred suspects. What you want is a one-paragraph sketch that describes *only* the person you are looking at.

Learning to Hear

If you are an eye person, like me, you may have a tendency to dismiss hearing as relatively unimportant. If that is so, try each of the three experiments that follow.

First, when a film you remember as exciting is shown on television, watch it with the sound off. Is it still exciting now? If not, why not?

The second is a thought-experiment; it would be difficult to do in the real world, and besides, it might get you killed. Imagine that by using some elaborate version of the hemispherical mufflers airport workers use, you could block out all sound from your ears. Now think of yourself getting up in the morning, putting on your mufflers, and going through a day's normal activities while completely deaf—walking or driving through traffic, crossing the street, etc.

For your third experiment, cover your eyes with a mask of some kind and sit in a room where other people are talking and moving about. How many different sounds are you hearing, and how do they affect you? How many were you aware of before you put the mask on? What is the difference, if any, between the way these sounds make you feel when your eyes are closed and the way they made you feel with your eyes open?

An Exercise in Hearing

Now write a scene in which several people are moving and talking:

1. from the viewpoint of a character whose eyes are open;
2. from the viewpoint of a blindfolded character.

Use the same actions, speeches, etc., in both versions.

This exercise may be of specific use to you later, if you ever write a scene involving a blind person, or a person in the dark. What is even more important is that it will strengthen your understanding of the way sounds influence people, particularly when they are under stress.

Learning to Remember

Most of the student writers I meet fall into two classes: those who have something to say but don't know how, and those who know how, to some degree, but have nothing to say. Members of this second group are oftener men than women. I sympathize with them, because I remember how hungry I was to write *anything* that would get published.

Something of the same sort happened when I was an art student. Drawing from life is essentially a mechanical process, and I learned to do it with some facility: I could draw anything you put in front of me in correct proportion and with all the details filled in, but I didn't value this skill because I could see perfectly well that my drawings were empty. There was nothing interpretive about them— they didn't mean anything.

If I had pursued a career in graphic art, I think I would have found out eventually the same thing I found out in writing. Looked at as a technical construct, a story is a shell built to contain something. What is marvelous about the shell is that it can capture and hold something so insubstantial as an image or a feeling.

After I had been writing for about fifteen years, I began to think seriously about the content of fiction, and I realized that for years, without knowing it, I had been storing up in my memory certain vivid moments that had and still have deep significance for me. Taken as a whole, my memory will never win any prizes; I forget dates, days of the week, old addresses, people's names; there are areas of my life that are completely blank. But these moments are as bright and sharp as ever, although some of them are now forty or fifty years old. I think that, even that long ago, my unconscious was reacting to those moments with the excitement and shock of revelation; and I think they contain the essential thing I am trying to capture in fiction.

Here is one of these memories. The bookkeeper in an office where I worked was a sour-faced woman in her late forties. When we went to her for our pay envelopes, she threw them on the desk and glared. She was the dark spot in that office. One afternoon, for the first time, I happened to ride down in the elevator with her; she was talking to someone else, smiling up at him, and I saw with a shock that she was beautiful. I had never seen her smile before. I realized that she was a person, the center of her own drama, not just a bit player in mine. Years later I began to understand why she could not smile in that office, why she led two lives.

Another: When I was in the third grade, one of the boys in my class had an epileptic fit. I saw him lying beside his desk, jerking, his limbs drawn up; I saw the blood from his bitten tongue. I must have thought it was a punishment: I used it that way, years later, in a story called "The Country of the Kind."

When I was interviewing some old friends for a book called *The Futurians,* I found out that some of them had these bright little fragments—"snapshots," I called them—and others didn't. There must be five or six different kinds of normal human memory. Maybe you don't have these vivid little snapshots, but if not, maybe you have some other kind of recollection that is just as filled with significance for you.

An Exercise in Remembering

Try to think of something in your childhood that you have remembered as mysterious and important. Don't force it; if it doesn't come up immediately, it probably will in a day or two. When you have this memory, think about it: try to understand why it seems to mean so much. Was this a moment when you first realized that someone you loved could be cruel—or that someone you hated could be warm and generous? Was this memory like a piece of a jigsaw puzzle that didn't fit—and if so, can you make it fit now? From this you may get an idea for a story, and if you do, it certainly will not be an empty shell.

Learning to Feel

As children we are vividly aware of our own feelings, but it never even occurs to us that others have feelings too, or that it matters whether they do or not. As we grow older we are exhorted to consider the feelings of others, and eventually we learn to do so, if only to improve our own opinion of ourselves. Real empathy comes later, and in some people never; but you can't be a mature artist without it.

Tolstoy, for one, writes so simply and convincingly about people of all ages and both sexes that you can't help feeling he is simply writing what he has experienced, although you know perfectly well Tolstoy has never been a young mother or a girl in love for the first time.

Not everybody can be Tolstoy, but if you hope to do even competently what he did supremely well, you must cultivate three things:

- acceptance of your own feelings
- observation of other people
- role-playing

The first sounds easy, but most people don't know what their real feelings are and are terrified of finding out. This is a consequence, and maybe a necessary one, of the training we have all had in suppressing various feelings and urges that our parents considered undesirable. We had to learn, for instance, to repress our rage when our little sister got a toy we wanted, to suppress the urge to hit her with a baseball bat or any handy weapon, and to suppress and *deny* the wish that she might be found dead the next morning. At the same time, each of us learns to suspect that he is the only one who has these shameful urges, the only one who doubts what he is told, the only one who does not behave well naturally, and since the weight of the evidence is against him, he concludes that he must be a monster.

It may take years to convince yourself that it is not a crime for you to feel the way you do. In the meantime, try looking at it this way: even if it *is* a crime to feel this way or that, human feelings are the basic stuff of fiction. Your own feelings are the only ones directly accessible to you, and therefore you must study them.

As a beginning, watch for those moments when some thought comes into your head and instantly clicks off, so fast sometimes that you don't even know what it was. Instead of looking the other way as you habitually do, think about that; try to recreate the way it felt when you had that thought: try to capture it again, and this time hold onto it and look at it. What was that thought, and why were you afraid of it?

Once you have the habit of observing your own feelings, you will be better equipped to interpret the signals other people give when they are feeling similar things. And when you have learned a little about that, you can do what Tolstoy did: you can put yourself in the place of another person, even one of the opposite sex and a different age, and feel what that person would feel.

Opportunities to practice imaginative role-playing will come to you often; you can't avoid them, unless you are a hermit. When two people you know are having an argument, try to identify first with one, then the other—what does it feel like to *be* that person? What would it be like to *be* that crying child, or that old woman feeding the pigeons?

Collaborating with Fred

Not long ago I had to consult a medical specialist, one of a class of people I was taught to look on with respect, if not awe. When we had finished our business, this man said, blushing and stammering, "I want to ask you something. Where do you get your ideas?" It was not a social question; he really, intensely, wanted to know.

Most writers have been asked this question often enough to have worked out a standard answer. Edward Albee says, "From Schenectady." My answer is, "Ideas are everywhere. If you're looking for something *all the time,* no matter what it is, you'll find it."

I don't think this answer satisfies people, although it is true as far as it goes. What they really want to know is, "How do you do this miraculous thing?" And there is no way to tell them; but I am going to tell you.

To begin with, your mind comes in two parts, the conscious part and the other one. Never mind where they are located in the brain. One may be in the right hemisphere and the other in the left (but I don't think so), or one may be in the frontal lobes and the other in the hindbrain. (I don't think that's right, either, although what it *feels* like to me is that the conscious, accessible part of my mind is in front and the other part in the back.)

"Unconscious" is a lousy term, by the way—it isn't unconscious, it just has trouble communicating. "The silent mind" would be better, maybe, or "the tongue-tied mind," but I prefer to call it "Fred."

The conscious mind is trained in linear, logical thinking—if A, then B and C, and so on. Fred works better in webs of association. The conscious mind can speak to Fred directly, but he can communicate only indirectly, through dreams, hunches, intuitions, and psychic nudges. It is as if there were a single unobstructed channel from the conscious to Fred, but a tortuous network of narrow channels coming the other way.

In most people, the two minds are like prisoners in adjoining cells who have never learned to use the means of communication they have. When Fred tries to say something, you repress it: "I don't want to think about that." Mental activity in most people is usually all conscious, all unconscious, or unconscious masquerading as conscious ("That will teach you," for instance, when they have just done something cruel to a child).

Now writing, like any art (and also very much like creative science and invention), is a thing you can't do without the close collaboration of the two parts of the mind. When you think about a creative problem, or even when you think something as simple as "I wish I had an idea for a story," you are sending a message to Fred. The return message may be in the form of a sudden realization, or an image, or some tantalizing ghost of an idea. It may come weeks or months later, even years.

The creative process is something like the growth of a crystal in a supersaturated solution—it takes time, and you must give it time. You can drop new seed crystals in now and then, and you can ask for and get glimpses of the product as it forms, but you can't force it beyond its own natural speed—parts have to come together, some of them from great psychic distances.

Fred will respond to your ideas pretty much the way you respond to the ideas you get from him: either a kind of dull, empty feeling, which means "No," or else an excitement, an electric tingle, that means "Yes, yes!"

In the early stages, you may have to teach Fred laboriously to understand what you want from him. "No, I can't put an elephant in the living room." "That's too simple—try again." And so on. Remember that learning to write is just as difficult for Fred as it is for you.

At some point, you must begin to use at least part of what Fred sends up. If you don't, he will become discouraged and indifferent, just as you would if nobody answered your letters or adopted your suggestions.

For the same reason, you should keep the appointments you make with Fred. If you say to yourself, for instance, "I'm going to write the drugstore scene tomorrow morning," you should do it. It is painful to Fred to get all the materials assembled and ready and then be forced to put off the work. But if Fred isn't ready, don't push. If you do, you are like a chess player who keeps telling his partner what moves to make. If that goes on long enough, of course your partner is going to say, "Well, play by yourself, then."

To be productive, Fred needs a lot of stimulating input—odd facts or fancies to knock together, insights, specimens, interesting data of all kinds. It took me a long time to realize this. I knew that every time I quit an editorial job I went into a highly productive period of writing, but I thought that was because I couldn't write while I held a job, and I was backlogged. That had something to do with it, but I believe now that I was responding to the *stimulus* of all those stories, good and bad, that I was reading critically in the office.

Being excited about some subject, reading a lot of books about it and going back and forth from one to another as I often do, has the same effect on me, and so does talking to other writers at a convention or workshop.

Critics talk about "the well of inspiration," and they say that the well sometimes runs dry. What this means, in my opinion, is either that the author is feeling the lack of stimulating input, or that she has not given Fred time enough to think about the problem. Trying to force this process is a mistake. Fred is as eager to work as you are, and when the dialogue is taking place it is an intensely pleasurable activity. I think Fred is as delighted by your succinct little formulations as you are by the nuggets of meaning Fred sends up. I think that accounts for the silences. When I have reduced some insight to a simple statement and dropped it back in, I think Fred says "Oh!" and falls silent in wonder. "How marvelous! I must think about that."

It is important to remember that there are things Fred can't do as well as you can. Fred is responsible for the images, the symbolism, the cloudy shapes of stories, but he can't fill in the practical details—that's your job. How does Lloyd get to Detroit when he has no car and no money? What makes Anita break her lunch date with Charley, even though she desperately needs to clear up their misunderstanding? Too often, beginning writers fail to do this conscious work of rationalization. They are right to trust Fred's assurance that the story means something, but they have forgotten that it must also make sense.

Like every rule, this one has exceptions. It is not true of surreal fiction—Kafka's stories, for instance. But stories written in a realistic mode—and that means most stories—must use a superficial daylight logic in order to get past the censor of the reader's conscious mind.

Beware of flashes of inspiration you get in dreams or in the half-waking state. Your censor is asleep then, and these ideas may seem absolutely brilliant until you try to put them into practice. Nevertheless, dreaming is good for some reason that I haven't figured out yet, and sleep is good because it makes the conscious mind *shut up* and gives Fred a chance to think. Drop an unsolved or half-solved problem in before bedtime; in the morning, chances are, you will see it in a different light.

An Exercise in Collaborating with Fred

1. Think of some germ for a story—a character, a situation, a vivid scene, or anything that appeals to you. Turn it over in your mind a little, trying to think of possible ways to develop it. When you reach a dead end, put the idea out of your mind. Your attitude should be one of patient waiting; you should have the expectation that after a while, maybe later in the day, or the next morning, Fred will signal that he has something to say about your idea. If this doesn't happen at first, continue to wait. Bring the idea back into your consciousness every now and then in a contemplative way, without trying to force it. This sends a polite signal to Fred that you are still interested: a sort of "How are you coming on that?"

2. When Fred does suggest something, it will be in the form of an idea that seems to pop into your head spontaneously. Be as accepting as you can. Even if the idea seems irrelevant, it may be part of a buried structure that is more important than the surface structure you know about.

3. Work consciously on the combination of ideas you now have until you are able to add something or take it a stage further. Put it out of your mind again.

4. Repeat steps 2 and 3 until the story is fully formed in your mind.

5. Begin writing the story. If at any point you feel you have "run dry" or are stopped for no apparent reason, again put the story out of your mind and wait for an idea to surface. Repeat this process until the story is finished.

Part 2

IDEA INTO STORY

Getting Ideas

If I had been a newspaper reporter, my doctor probably would have said, "You must meet a lot of interesting people," but he would not have asked where I got my ideas. A reporter simply writes about something that happens. But fiction is written "out of the author's head," and that makes it mysterious.

I have already described how fiction comes from a dialogue between the conscious and unconscious minds. But who starts the conversation? I suspect that very often, by the time the writer becomes aware that she has a story idea, the dialogue has already been going on so long that it's impossible to remember who started it.

When you have been writing for some time, it is probable that most of your ideas will come "spontaneously." Sometimes they are more than ideas—they are full-fledged stories that have only to be written down. My story "Not with a Bang" came to me during the time it took for a men's-room door to close behind me in a Swedish restaurant in New York. I didn't have the characters or the setting, but I had the whole structure; all I needed was to find parts to fit.

There may be times, especially in the beginning, when you will want to begin the dialogue yourself. There are many ways to do this, and they all work. It really doesn't seem to matter what the initial input is—it is just a starting point, like the grain of sand around which an oyster makes a pearl.

Years ago I noticed that the running heads in a reference volume, *The Index to the Science Fiction Magazines,* sometimes formed coherent phrases. I wrote stories around two of these. One was a long story called "Stranger Station." What the phrase suggested to me was a space satellite designed to receive visitors from other planets. I dropped that into the unconscious, and images of cold, isolation, and alienness began coming back. The story developed out of these.

By this time, I think, I had trained Fred to be on the lookout for odd bits of information or experience that could be made into stories; whenever he found one, he would give me a signal that I recognized—a sort of electric tingle. I felt the tingle when I saw a sign, "Ticket to Anywhere," in the movie version of Geoffrey Household's *Rogue Male*. It was just a sign over the ticket window in a British railway station, but I read it literally, and it gave me a story about an alien transportation system, abandoned by its makers thousands of years ago. It would take you from one planet to another in an instant, but you couldn't choose your destination—you were buying a "ticket to anywhere."

I got the idea for a novel, *A for Anything,* from a newspaper story about a prizefighter who had been a member of a street gang in his youth. He said they would steal anything that began with "A": *a* bicycle, *a* radio, *a* tape recorder, etc. The title came from this; then I had to explain it, which I did by imagining a device that would copy anything—bicycles, radios, even people.

These stories came out of a kind of wordplay; other stories have come from play with ideas and situations. In the 1960s, when I was living in Kentucky, a neighbor of mine had a back porch full of garbage; he wouldn't carry it out to the road until the garbage collectors picked up what he had, and they wouldn't pick it up until he carried it out to the road. Obviously some third solution was needed. I suggested that he bag the stuff neatly and put it in a roadside stand under a sign: "Garbage, 25¢ a bag." He didn't take my suggestion (eventually his wife dumped all the garbage into his pickup), but I transformed it by an easy association (garbage and manure) into a science-fiction story in which aliens from another planet start a boom in cowpats: it was called "The Big Pat Boom."

Another way of generating a story idea is to turn some conventional idea on its head. In science fiction, for example, there had been a number of stories about the one immortal person in a world of mortals. I turned this upside down and got a long story called "The Dying Man."

Still another way is to notice what is being left out by the writers of conventional fiction, and concentrate on that. When I was young, one of the standard characters in science-fiction stories was the granite-jawed hero who was never afraid of anything. There were good reasons for that, at the time—those stories were written for adolescents who wanted to escape from their own fears. But if you pretend that fear doesn't exist, you are ignoring a big part of the spectrum of human emotion and one of the strongest forces behind our behavior. I wrote about my fear of heights *(A for Anything)*, of drowning ("The Dying Man"), of mutilation ("Masks"), and even about my fear of being afraid ("Time Enough").

Somebody once said that there is a story in every tombstone. There are stories in newspaper articles and even in the notices in the back pages—births and deaths, marriages and divorces, bankruptcies, court cases.

Almost anything you see around you can be magically transformed into material for fiction. Children do this, turning twigs into forests or dirt into mountains. Most grownups have forgotten how, and yet it's very simple. Look at the object as if it were different in some way—bigger, smaller, made of some other material, etc. At the same time, look at the object as if *you* were not your everyday self but somebody else with a special interest in that object—a Martian, for instance, or a detective, or a fetishist, as in the first three of these examples:

Let's say you are looking at your foot. How can you make a story out of that?

• A science-fiction story about an alien whose feet are not like ours. (How are they different, and why? To answer these questions, you will have to invent the whole alien, and the planet she comes from, and her culture, and so on. Then, why is she here? Once you have all this background, you will be well on the way to a story.)

• A mystery story involving a footprint left by someone with a deformed foot. (Deformed in what way? When and how? Is the person who left the footprint the murderer or not? Where is the footprint, and what was that person doing there? And so on.)

• An erotic story about a foot-fetishist. (What sort of feet does he like, and why? What does he do to gratify his desire? How do his love-objects respond to him?)

- A love story about a well-dressed young man who attracts the attention of a waitress by coming into a restaurant barefoot. (Is this just one of a series of bizarre things he does? Might be fun.)
- An adventure story about someone who is forced by circumstances to walk through the snow barefoot on a freezing night. (Why? Where does she have to go? What happens?)
- A Cinderella story about a young woman who wears a 4½ shoe. (Who is Prince Charming in the story—a photographer looking for the perfect foot?)

Another way is to open a small paperback dictionary, choose a word at random, then do it again and find another. What do the two words, taken together, remind you of? Vonda N. McIntyre's award-winning novel *Dreamsnake* came from a similar exercise at the Clarion Workshop.

When you have an idea, you're not done: the idea is not the story. But it's pretty hard to write a good story without at least one; more often it takes two or three.

Let me illustrate by talking about two ideas I gave other writers when I was an editor. One was called "The Mindworm"; it was about a creature who could read your mind like a book. I mentioned this to Cyril Kornbluth, and he put it together with the idea of the vampire to make a classic story. The other was just a speculation: what if it turned out that a number of people in the same town were dreaming the same dreams? Kate Wilhelm combined this with the idea of the collective unconscious of a dying town, and made it into "Somerset Dreams," one of her most memorable stories. In both cases it was the second idea that made the story work.

Some Confessions

When I was about fifteen, I knew that I wanted to write stories, but I didn't know how. One way I tried that didn't work was just to think of a first sentence and then go on from there. Once, I remember, I started something like this. (Actually, I'm pretty sure it was worse than this.)

> Grando Marco, Emperor of the Martian Confederacy, sat
> on his throne and looked out the window at the setting sun.

That was as far as I got. I had only the vaguest idea who Grando Marco was, etc., and the more I thought about it the more I couldn't think of anything.

A few years later, when I was eighteen or nineteen, I wanted to write a story about an alien invasion. It was going to be a quiet invasion, without heat rays or explosions, and that was not a bad idea, but I picked it too green. Again, I started off with a sentence or two, hoping something would suggest itself.

> Long after midnight, Millie Horst was awake in her tenement room. The pain had been worse than usual that night.

Again the story died, because I had no idea what to do with Millie Horst, and only the vaguest notion of what the alien invaders were up to. Actually, I had thought of the second idea that could have made the first one work, but I didn't notice it. Millie Horst was nothing but an observer—she was going to be the first one to see the aliens landing, or whatever—after that she had nothing to do.

Suppose I had had the wit to tie the two elements together? I might have had the aliens zap Millie with n-rays that would have stopped her pain and changed her personality, making her an aggressive and dynamic person. Would she have become some sort of collaborator of the aliens, or would she have led the fight to destroy them? Either way, there could have been a story there—not a very good story, and I wouldn't try to write it now, but at least a story that I could have finished, and in those days I might have sold it.

Remember my two-page, single-spaced story about the Martians who encoded their minds in a computerlike device and waited for explorers from Earth to find it? When I was about twenty I dragged this story out again and added another idea to it. This time the central character was the son of the leader of the first expedition to the planet (it wasn't Mars this time). The first expedition hadn't come back, and the hero and his crew were sent to find out why. After some hugger-mugger he did so, and rescued his father (who was in suspended animation) *and* revived the aliens (who were in suspended animation too), and the whole thing wound up in a blaze of good fellowship. It was a bad story, it was about seven thousand words long, and I sold it to a magazine for half a cent a word.

I'm telling you these embarrassing anecdotes about myself for two reasons. I want you to realize that no matter how awful your work is now, it can't be any worse than mine was; and I want to show you some of the ways by which I finally climbed out of the mire.

In my late twenties, when I was a published writer and should have known better, I tried to write a story about another single idea—a computer that could write fiction. The idea itself was all that interested me, and I tried to disguise it as a story by having mysterious artworks of various kinds appear anonymously here and there (the computer could draw, too), while the viewpoint character wondered what was going on. The story lay down and stopped breathing after about a thousand words.

Twenty years later I tried again. I had had a chance to think about the fiction-writing computer in the meantime, and I realized that I didn't believe in it, but I did believe in a computer program that would write fiction in collaboration with a human operator. He became my central character—not the mysterious inventor skulking in the background, but a simple IBM employee.

My concern this time was not just to set forth the original idea—the story-writing computer—but to explore the society that would have to exist around it. I decided that it would be a sanitized and conformist world, and I learned from Fred, somewhat to my surprise, that it was a world in which the blacks in North America had been exterminated in a race war, and the survivors were carrying a load of subconscious guilt. It was this second idea that made the story work. (It was called "Down There.") The story-writing computer had become an emblem of an alienated, dehumanized, plastic society in which everything spontaneous had been suppressed, beginning with the blacks, who were perceived as dangerously "natural."

When you have established a working relationship between your conscious and unconscious minds ("Down There" is a metaphor for this collaboration, by the way, and the whole story is really about the unconscious), you can trust your partner to come up with suggestions that will vitalize the story, whether they seem relevant at first or not.

Manipulating Ideas

Let's say now that you have some sort of vague idea for a story. Where do you go from there?

Particularize. You can't write about a general character in a general setting—you need a particular person in a particular place, feeling a particular way, in a particular situation. Suppose, for instance, that what you start with is an emotion—a mixture of fear and anxiety, let's say. Who is feeling this emotion? You decide that it's a young woman. Where is she? In a mountain cabin, alone, at night. And so on. (The next thing you will want to decide is who's out there that makes her feel that way.)

When you have chosen a character, you have made a choice that will determine the success or failure of your story—either it is a character whom you understand and for whom you feel affection, or it isn't. (Love and understanding are the missing ingredients in most slushpile stories. If you don't understand your character, you can't make her believable, and if you don't care about her, the reader won't either.)

Complicate the story by introducing another character, or some event or circumstance that makes the outcome more uncertain and therefore more interesting. Let's say that you need a third character in the story about the mountain cabin. Is it a boy delivering groceries, or a lawyer, or a doctor, or a sheriff's deputy investigating a crime? Each time you answer a question like this, you will be closer to finding out *what happens* in the story.

It took me years of stubborn effort, by the way, to find out that I couldn't write a plotted story with only one character, even when the environment was so important to the story that it could be considered a second character. I think there are two reasons for this. First, if you put a character into a story all alone, she tends to spend a lot of time looking into her own navel. Second, if you write using only one character, you lose the opportunity to define that character by the way she responds to other characters, and vice versa.

In "Stranger Station," I had a human being and an alien in a space satellite, but the alien was behind a bulkhead and it never spoke, never acted; it was just there—part of the background. The story wouldn't go until I introduced a third character, an intelligent computer, referred to by the protagonist as "Aunt Jane." When the protagonist dies, Aunt Jane is left behind, and the story has a resonance; it seems to go on past the ending on the page.

For a better-known example, see Jack London's "To Build a Fire." You may remember this as a pure story of "man against nature"—a man trying to survive alone in the subzero cold of the Arctic. But there is a third character in London's story—the dog. He has the survival knowledge that the man lacks; when the man dies, the dog goes on, and our sympathy goes with him. The dog gives the story its resonance, and makes it possible for us to accept the man's death.

Editors are often reluctant to publish any short story that ends with the death of a sympathetic viewpoint character, and with good reason—see "The Implied Contract," p. 54. Such an ending can be softened by a last-minute change to the viewpoint of another character who survives: then the reader becomes a mourner rather than the corpse.

The third character is useful in still another way, to keep your plots from being too simple. Often the minor conflicts between allies are more interesting than the head-to-head conflict between enemies. Whenever you have three characters feeling intensely about the same thing, seeing it in three completely different ways, and each one right by his own standards, you can be pretty sure that you have material for a strong story.

Criticize the story as you go along. How did that elephant get in the living room? (Never mind where it came from—how did it get through the *door*?) How old is this child, and why is she talking like a five-year-old on page 2, and a teenager on page 3? *Why* does your hero, a timid bank teller, suddenly go out into the jungle stalking a tiger?

By asking yourself these questions now, you will save yourself the embarrassment of having others ask them later.

Experience

"Write what you know," young writers are often told, and there is a little something to this. Generally speaking, I think young people whose sexual and emotional experience is still limited ought to put off writing about love and marriage. If you have never had a job, you probably can't write convincingly about people in an office or factory.

Details of the way people dress, talk, and behave in various places and in various situations are immensely valuable to a writer, and for that reason I think it is a mistake for anybody to go straight from school into writing, without any contact at all with the real world.

But please don't think you should prepare yourself by working on a shrimp boat, in a sawmill, as a dealer in Las Vegas, or any of those neat things that you read about on the backs of book jackets. Sometimes this kind of work experience pays off and sometimes not. Mark Twain wrote one little story, not a very good one, about riverboat pilots, none about the Civil War, one—not his best— about apprentice printers. But he knew people—all kinds of people—and that gave him all the material for writing he needed. That's why I'm telling you that you ought to have *some* experience of the world ordinary people live in before you commit yourself to a career as a writer. The chances are that life will force these experiences on you anyhow, but if you have a choice, think carefully before you skip all that.

Having said this much, I now have to tell you that firsthand experience isn't enough. You can't be a lawyer, a doctor, a firefighter, a farmer, and a housewife—life is too short. The most valuable thing you can learn is how to use your own experiences to help you project yourself in imagination into the lives of other people. Write what you know,* by all means, when you can, but fill in the spaces by *finding out* what you need to know.

Research

When you have decided to write a story involving a subject about which you are ignorant—astrophysics, let's say—how much should you find out about that subject before you begin? You probably expect me to say "all you can," but I won't. It would take a lifetime to find out all you can learn about astrophysics, or even about Akron, Ohio. Instead, you should try to find out all you need to know for the purposes of the story, and no more. If you don't impose that limit, you are likely to get bogged down in endless research and never write the story. Or, if you write it, you will feel an irresistible urge to cram all that information in, and it will anchor your story down like the buckshot in Mark Twain's jumping frog.

An example: When I was planning the story "The Dying Man," I wanted a plausible way to extend human life indefinitely. I looked up "Aging" in the encyclopedia, and found out a little something about hormones and connective tissue, but that was not what I wanted. One of the charts in the article caught my eye, and after I thought about it I realized that it had given me a general answer to the problem. What the chart showed was that homo sap has a much longer juvenile period in relation to its life span than any other animal. What if that long slope of growth were lengthened still further and turned into an asymptotic curve, approaching maturity by smaller and smaller amounts but never getting there? Then, barring disease, accident, and violence, people would never mature and therefore would never age and die.

---

*Taken literally, this injunction would make all historical fiction, all science fiction, and all fantasy impossible. What would Homer, Milton, Dante, or Shakespeare have thought of it?

If, instead of this, I had insisted on a technical answer to the problem, I could have read a dozen or a hundred books on aging, longevity, human genetics, and biochemistry, and, since I still would have had to make up the answer, it probably would have come out like this: "It all hinges on the metabolization of L-dopa-acetylcholine 1,2,19 by trimethylphosphate B. *Extremely* complicated." This is garbage, of course, and it would not have informed my readers who knew nothing about biochemistry, or improved the tempers of those who did.

Library research is indispensable, but it does not take the place of thought, and it has other limitations. More often than not, the one little piece of information you want is missing from the literature. Then you have to find an expert; but do the library research first, so that you can ask the right questions. Kate Wilhelm once needed to know how long it takes a killer whale calf to be born. She read books about whales, and learned many interesting things, but not that. She went to a whale expert at an aquatarium, and he not only told her the answer (twenty minutes), but talked to her about whales for three hours without a break for lunch.

If you get your information aurally, and if it is at all technical, make sure you know how to spell the words. Do not emulate a friend of a friend of mine, who questioned a doctor in Brooklyn by telephone about neurosurgery and wound up writing "innovation" for "innervation."

Using Constraints

A constraint is something that limits what you can do; for example, rhyme, meter, and form are constraints in poetry; if you are writing a sonnet, it can't have more or less than fourteen lines. Character, setting, and situation are all constraints in fiction. If your central character is a deeply moral and law-abiding person, there are a lot of things she can't do—she can't embezzle money from her employer, for instance. If the setting is a small town in Arizona, your native characters can't talk or behave like Park Avenue millionaires.

If your character is a nineteenth-century explorer adrift on an ice floe in the Arctic, he can't pick up the telephone and call for help.

The more you know about your characters, setting, and situation, the more constraints there are—and the *easier* it becomes to decide what can and will happen in the story. To test this, imagine trying to write a story in which anything is possible. Your central character can be a man one moment and a woman the next; she can be in Bloomingdale's on page 1 and on top of Mount Anapurna on page 2. This freedom may sound exhilarating, but try it and see how long it takes you to become bored and disgusted. On a less extravagant scale, you may have done this already—you may have tried to write a story about a character you knew very little about, and found that you couldn't imagine what she would do. Constraints are your friends because they limit the possibilities to a number small enough to handle.

Here is a character in the middle of a featureless desert. He can go north, south, east, or west; there are no constraints on his movements. There is no story here because it doesn't *matter* what he does.

Here is another character at the bottom of a well. The well has caved in above him. Here there is no story because there are too many constraints on his movements; he can't go anywhere.

Now here is a character in a maze. Each time she passes through an intersection, a door closes behind her. One route leads to her goal; all the others are dead ends. Here we have just enough constraints, not too many or too few.

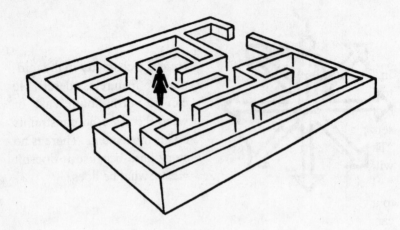

The Quadrangle: Character, Setting, Situation, Emotion

In the story about the young woman alone in the mountain cabin, we began with an emotion, a mixture of fear and anxiety; from that we got a character, the young woman, a setting, the mountain cabin; and a situation—she is alone, at night, and there's something or somebody out there. All four of these things are still undeveloped, but they are there, and we have the necessary underpinnings of a story. We have pegged it down at all four corners, like a tent.

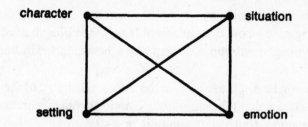

Notice that you can begin from any corner of the quadrangle. In "Not with a Bang," I began with a situation—a man condemned to death by the closing of a men's-room door. Emotion was implied by this; character and setting came later. In "Stranger Station," the setting came first—the vast, empty space-station. In a story called "The Cage," I began with a character—an aging postal employee with a secret.

Even when you begin with an abstract idea, you must follow it to a character, a setting, a situation, and an emotion before there can be a story. In "Mary," for instance, I began with an idea—romantic love as an outdated obsession. From this I went to character, setting, and situation; again, the emotion took care of itself.

Another Example

This time, let's say, you're thinking about an orphan who has found a loaded revolver in a garbage can. That's an intriguing situation, but you have no idea where to go from there.

Try making a list of four things the orphan might do next. If you write down the first four things you think of, maybe they come out something like this:

- Hold up a liquor store
- Kill somebody
- Kill himself
- Throw the gun away

Now cross out all four. Think of the fifth solution, the one that is not *obvious*.

Suppose your fifth solution is:

• Give it to somebody

All right, to whom does he give it? Out of the silent half of your mind an image swims up: a woman who is being abused by her husband.

Now you have a sense of what the emotional charge of the story will be. (If you don't feel any strong emotion about this ending, it's the wrong one; find a sixth solution, or a seventh.)

The rough form of the story gives you two things that are tentatively established, although you may change them later: The story takes place in an urban setting. The central character has no family (an orphan) and no job or other means of support, or he wouldn't be looking in garbage cans.

Notice that at this stage, everything in the story except its basic form is in suspension. You are going back and forth between the corners of the quadrangle, changing this and that, hoping for improvement or inspiration.

What if, instead of a big city, the setting is a small town? Think of the town, and your character in it. Where does he sleep? What sort of town is it? What is the landscape? Follow your character in imagination through one whole day, visualizing the settings and the people he meets. Are the woman and her cruel husband among them? Probably not, and that's too bad, because the orphan must be able to observe them closely over a long period, or the story won't work. Say that he rents a room in their apartment, where he often sees the man beating and terrorizing the woman.

But why doesn't he interfere? How can he afford to rent a room and still be reduced to looking for food in garbage cans?

Now you see, in a flash of illumination, that he isn't an orphan and he isn't a derelict: He is a member of the family, perhaps the man's younger brother. That's why he lives there, and why he doesn't interfere. The older brother gives him a room but won't feed him; the younger brother is reduced to eating kitchen scraps from garbage cans in the alleys outside restaurants. (Is the town too small to have more than one restaurant? Let's make it bigger.)

At this point, perhaps for the first time, you can begin to think seriously about your characters. They must be people who will naturally and inevitably do what you want them to do, and they must belong to their own background and their own past. How does the older brother dominate the other two so completely? If the wife is abused, why doesn't she leave? Is she an invalid?

Whatever you decide about the characters, don't make the mistake of carving them out solely to do what you want them to: Characters constructed to do only one thing are wooden. What *else* do they do? What are their individual quirks, interests, virtues and failings? When you can see the characters and hear them talk, you may find they want to say or do something you had not intended. That's a good sign. Accommodate them if you can.

If you have done this work carefully, even the monster that we have made of the older brother will be believable, and so will the ending. The central character does not have the courage to kill his brother himself, but he hands the gun to the woman and then goes away, leaving the reader with a resonance of bitterness, regret, perhaps a touch of horror.

Notice that at any moment in this process, one of the parts you started with may unmask itself as one that doesn't fit. There is a story by H. G. Wells about an eastern potentate who orders a temple built around the sarcophagus of his dead wife. He continually alters the plans; the building becomes more and more magnificent as it rises. One day he notices the small dark object at its center, and frowns.

"Take that thing away," he says.

Theme

You may be thinking that if the quadrangle is a tent, it ought to have a tent pole in the middle. You're quite right, and here it is.

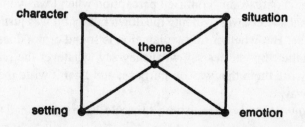

The reason I didn't put this in earlier is that I have a strong prejudice against beginning with a theme. Looking back at stories I have done, I can see perfectly well that some of them have themes; in "Down There," for instance, the story says that anything repressed in the psyche will return in another form. But I didn't start with that or any other theme, and I was not conscious of it while I wrote. I knew it was there, all right, but I also knew that if I let it come up to consciousness I would start trying to elaborate it in mechanical, linear ways, and it would be a clunker.

What usually happens when a writer deliberately begins with a theme is that it overwhelms everything else. For one thing, it becomes painfully obvious that the characters are not self-employed but are working for the author, doing what she tells them to.

Your characters are your employees, and your readers know that, but if you are adroit and lucky you can make them forget it temporarily. The last thing you want to do is rub their noses in it.

Imagine for a moment what it would be like if *your* life had a theme imposed by some celestial author, obliging you at a certain point to make an impassioned speech about human rights, for instance, when your natural inclination is to go and have lunch.

Character, setting, situation, and emotion will often generate a theme. It may not be the one that would have occurred to you if you had felt obliged to know your theme in the beginning.

Over a period of time you may find your stories saying again and again something you didn't know you intended to say. It is just as well not to worry about this, because it will happen whether you do or not. My stories, for example, say over and over, in different ways, that even a monster has the right to struggle for life. "Masks" is an example of this, and so are "Down There," "Stranger Station," "The Country of the Kind," and many others. I think this comes from a reaction to my confused perception when I was young, not only that society was grinding me down but that it was justified in doing so. But whether this explanation is sound or not doesn't really matter; my stories say what they say, whatever the reason. I don't write them that way on purpose, and I can't write them any other way.

Many critics, beginning with Aristotle, have maintained that the purpose of fiction is to instruct people in right action—teach them how to behave, in other words. This seems a little too restrictive to me, although I suppose you could say that in any story the characters are behaving either correctly or incorrectly, and if you care to you can draw a moral from that. But the most interesting stories to me are those in which people are behaving in morally ambiguous ways, so that it's not easy to say that what they're doing is right or wrong.

I'm telling you where I stand so that you can allow for my bias. Other writers—and you may be one of them—prefer stories that demonstrate the correctness of the Ten Commandments, the Golden Rule, or some other conventional code of conduct. And of course some readers also like these stories; but they tend to age rapidly, because conventional attitudes change. Fiction of this kind written only forty years ago already looks a little quaint. What seems to me much more interesting and more likely to endure is the story that does not try to prescribe conduct but only to describe it honestly. And this brings me to my point: I think readers of serious fiction are always looking, on some level, for information about what the world is really like—what it means to be human, what it's all about. Any honest answer to this is a good answer, whether it looks like a "theme" or not.

Meaning

One of the reasons I would not let myself think about the theme of "Down There," maybe, is that what I was really after was meaning, not theme; if I had fixed my attention on theme, I might have lost the meaning.

I know what I mean by *meaning,* but it is not easy to explain. I don't mean *intention,* which is implied by the verb *mean* in this sentence; I mean a quality in fiction that is felt in the work as a whole, cannot be separated from it, and gives the reader a feeling of illumination or revelation. *Meaning* in this sense and *theme* are not the same thing. You can extract the theme from a story and condense it into a single sentence; you can't do that with meaning. Theme is something you can look at directly, but you can see meaning only out of the corner of your eye. A story contains meaning (like a jug) but exhibits a theme (like a billboard). John Cheever's "The Swimmer," for instance, is intensely meaningful, but I don't see that it has a theme, unless it is something as banal as "Spendthrifts come to grief," or "Youth is fleeting." Other stories have both meaning and theme, and there are some that have themes but no meaning that I can see.

I wrote a lot of stories when I was young that were fun for me and the reader but didn't mean anything especially. I didn't have anything to say about the lives of my characters because I didn't understand my own life then. I was doing the best I could with what I had, and I'm not ashamed of those stories now.

If you are a young writer, and if all this talk about "meaning" strikes you as mystical or incomprehensible, that's okay. Maybe it will make sense to you later, and even if it never does, you may have a happy and successful career writing stories that are fun to read.

What Is a Story?

To begin with, all writing is a device to encode the writer's thoughts into a communication that can be decoded by a reader and turned back into thoughts again. When this works, the reader's sense of direct communication is an illusion, like the voice you hear in a telephone. (The sounds you hear are made by magnetic diaphragms stimulated by electric impulses; your friend's voice is not even speaking at the exact moment you think you hear it.) One rather sad consequence is that a given utterance may be alive for some reader when it is dead for the author. In such cases, when the reader and the author meet in person, there is a baffled sense that one of them has come at the wrong time. Upsetting as this is, it is one of the most important advantages we have. We may not be the only species that is thinking about itself—maybe cats spend their idle time thinking about catness—but we are almost certainly the only terrestrial species that is encoding its thoughts in order to communicate them from one generation to another.

The difficulties of this kind of translation are many and great, but it is difficulties that make art. Moreover, it is the specific difficulties of the medium that give any art its typical character. (Compare a sculpture carved in granite and one cast in bronze.) The more you learn to seek out difficulties and overcome them, the better your stories will be.

Nonfiction is expected to be true rather than entertaining, and fiction is expected to be entertaining rather than true. The difference is that in fiction, truth is presented in the form of an invention. All fiction, by definition, is a lie, but if it does not contain some truth it is shoddy.

Because fiction is an invention, the author has more freedom to make it esthetically satisfying than she does in nonfiction, and therefore our expectations of being gratified in this way are high. A successful story is or seems to be all of a piece—all in harmony, all saying the same thing in different ways, having its own steady rhythm, with nothing out of key, nothing inappropriate or irrelevant.

In a story we expect a quality of completion, of roundedness, which sets it apart from a sketch, an incident, or an anecdote. For example, this is a sketch:

A little boy, named Joe, who haunts about the bar-room and the stoop, about four years old, in a thin short jacket, and full-breeched trowsers, and bare feet. The men plague him, and put quids of tobacco in his mouth, under pretence of giving him a fig, and he gets enraged, and utters a peculiar sharp, spiteful cry, and strikes at them with a stick, to their great mirth. He is always in trouble, yet will not keep away. They dispatch him with two or three cents, to buy candy, and nuts and raisins. They set him down in a nitch of the door, and tell him to remain there a day and a half; he sits down very demurely, as if he really meant to fulfil his penance;— but, a moment after, behold there is little Joe, capering across the street to join two or three boys who are playing in a wagon.

The American Notebooks of Nathaniel Hawthorne

This is an incident:

Bill was a sophisticated college junior, and I was only a senior in high school when we went on our first date. After the movie, he suggested we go to Green Hill Park—a local lovers' lane—to look at the stars, but I murmured some excuse.

I found myself liking Bill more and more, but on the second date I still refused to go "look at the stars."

On the third date I finally agreed. Bill stopped the car in an isolated spot. I closed my eyes as his face came close to mine, but I opened them quickly as I heard his voice in my ear. "Now over there," he was saying, "that's Sagittarius. . . ."

Joan P. Fouhy, in *Reader's Digest*

The following is an anecdote:

The story goes that Mrs. Vanderbilt once demanded to know what Fritz Kreisler would charge to play at a private musicale, and was taken aback when he named a price of five thousand dollars. She agreed reluctantly, but added, "Please remember that I do not expect you to mingle with the guests." "In that case, Madam," Kreisler assured her, "my fee will be only two thousand."

Bennett Cerf, in *Try and Stop Me*

Finally, this is a story:

The last man on Earth sat alone in a room. There was a knock on the door. . . .

Anonymous

As you can see, the sketch is merely a vivid bit of description; the incident is something that happened, and so is the anecdote, with the difference that it is attached to a real person who is mentioned by name. The story, although it is only two sentences long, is complete by implication and is charged with meaning in a way that none of the others are.

The last sentence of Hawthorne's note, which I omitted before, reads as follows:

> Take this boy as the germ of a tavern-haunter, a country roué, to spend a wild and brutal youth, ten years of his prime in the States-Prison, and his age in the poor-house.

Now you can see how the sketch could have been expanded into a story, or even a novel, following the blighted life of the little boy who played around the barroom. The story might be told from the viewpoint of a childless man who takes pity on Joe and tries to help him, only to watch him follow his inevitable course.

In a similar way, the incident or the anecdote could be turned into a story by adding complications and characters. For example:

The high-school girl realizes that her stargazing boyfriend is too shy to kiss her, although she now wants to be kissed. The shyer he is, the more she loves him, but she can't make the first move herself because he might be alarmed by her aggressiveness. What stratagems does she employ, and which one finally works?

The violinist (we wouldn't call him Fritz Kreisler) is an aging virtuoso torn between his art and his desire to please his family by moving upward in society. In the end he chooses art in this dramatic way.

The last-man story, although it is complete as it stands, could be expanded to normal story length in the same way: the Earth has been conquered by aliens; they have killed off all animal life on the planet except for a few zoo specimens; the hero, the last man, is one of these. He has two problems—how to get rid of the aliens, and how to persuade the last *woman* to become the mother of the new human race. Fredric Brown actually wrote this one; he called it "Knock."

What do all four of these pieces have in common now that they didn't have before? In each one we have established an *emotional relationship* involving at least two people (Joe and the man who tries to help him; the high-school girl and her boyfriend; the violinist and his family; the last man and the last woman), and an impediment to a satisfactory conclusion (Joe's environment and his early life; the boyfriend's shyness; the violinist's love for his family; the last man's imprisonment in the alien zoo).

Look at your story idea: is it really nothing more than a sketch, an incident, or an anecdote? If so, make it into a story by adding an emotional involvement and an impediment. If you don't, the manuscript will come back with a note from the editor: "This isn't a story, it's a sketch (or an incident, or an anecdote)."

The Implied Contract

There is an implied contract between the author and the reader that goes something like this: Give me your time and pay your money, and I'll let you experience what it's like to be
- a trapper in the North Woods
- an explorer in the Martian desert
- a young woman in love with an older man
- a dying cancer patient . . .

You must look hard at the offer you are making: would you accept it, if *you* were the reader?

Most people have emotional problems of their own that hurt so much that they keep trying to push them down. Fiction can lure them into a vicarious experience that discharges these emotions. But you can't say, "Read this story, it will wring your guts." You have to say, "Read this story, it will interest and entertain you," and *then* wring their guts.

I see a lot of dying cancer patients in student work, probably because young writers think they are expected to be serious and grim. I read these stories for professional reasons, but if, when I'm reading for pleasure, I open a story and find that it's about some-body hopelessly ill with cancer, I am propelled out of that story by a reaction so automatic and swift that it's over before I can think about it.

There is a story by Algis Budrys, "Be Merry," that happens to be told from the viewpoint of a character who is dying of cancer. But he has come to terms with it, he is still mobile and function-ing, and in the story it doesn't matter. The character in Budrys's story can do something. The dying cancer patients in the stories I talked about above can't do anything. That's the difference.

Remember that you have no legislative power to make anybody read what you write. You are involved in a transaction with the reader; if you want her to read, you must offer her some compen-sation. ("Consideration" is what the lawyers call this, and no con-tract is valid without it.)

Building Blocks

Under the surface of every manuscript—the words and sentences—are a lot of other things that can't be seen, like the part of a build-ing that is under the floor. I didn't understand this when I began trying to write; I thought you just began with a sentence and then wrote another sentence, and so on, and I couldn't figure out why that wasn't working.

I don't think I caught on until I went to art classes when I was eighteen, and found out about preliminary drawings. When you want to produce a painting, you don't just pick up a brush and start; you make a drawing first, more likely a lot of drawings, until you get the composition right, and the balance of masses and lights and darks, and so on.

It's like that in writing too. Here is a stack of blocks, with "Sur-face" on the top. That's where I was trying to write stories, instead of building them from the bottom up. So let's begin at the bottom.

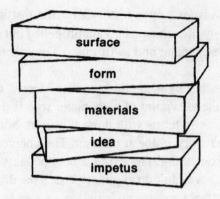

"Impetus" is the force that makes you want to write this story in the first place. If that force is just the desire to get published, or make money, or to "be a writer," the story will probably be weak. Of course you want to get published, and you'd like to make money, and you want to be a writer, but that's not enough. Strong stories are made from things that are inside you wanting to get out.

Then comes "Idea," or maybe it comes first—some general notion of a story you might write.

Next is "Materials." That means all the things you have to get together to build a story: characters, background, setting, and so on.

Then comes "Form," which is the shape of the thing you're making. Is it going to be a poem, or a short story, or a novel? Will it be simple and smooth, or intricate and knobby?

And finally "Surface," which is all the reader sees at first. But all these other things have to be underneath, or the story won't work.

This is a good thing to remember in workshops. If the story fails at any level, it's no use criticizing it at a higher level. If the story is wrong at the level of "Materials," for instance, it will fail no matter how good the form and the surface are. To criticize the story effectively, find the earliest level where it fails and try to fix it there. Are the characters made of cardboard? Then the dialogue is going to be weak, and there's no use trying to fix it at the dialogue level: You must make the characters real first. Then the dialogue, very likely, will be real too.

An Exercise in Story Building

Think of an idea for a story that for some reason you don't intend to write—perhaps because it's a kind of story that interests you as a reader but not as a writer. Build the foundations of the story from "Idea" up. When you get to "Surface," write a few lines of the opening and then stop.

I don't advise you to do this more than once or twice (you don't want to get into the habit of constructing stories and not writing them), but you can learn a good deal about story construction fairly easily by doing this exercise, because your investment in it is small and therefore you can take as many risks as you like.

Form

If you were to watch an artist making a pencil sketch, you might not know at first what her intentions were, but as she went on you would begin to get a glimpse of her design, and when she was finished, you would see what she had been working toward all along; you would realize that each apparently aimless stroke of her pencil had formed part of the shape.

A story has a shape, too; you can't see it all at once, but it's there. A good story has a pleasing shape, like a vase or a violin; a bad one has a meaningless, haphazard shape, like a pile of junk.

What the violin has that the pile of junk lacks is coherence, symmetry, and proportion. Coherence means that all the parts fit together; symmetry means that one mass is balanced by another. Think of the parts of stories in terms of balance: beginnings are balanced by endings (not only the beginning and ending of the story, but the beginning and ending of smaller parts, right down to the paragraph and the sentence). Slow is balanced by swift, sweet by sour, dark by light.

Proportion means that all the parts are in the same scale—the scroll of the violin, for instance, is not twice the size of the sound box; the beginning of a story is not twice as long as all the rest put together.

When you write stories by a random process, trying this and that to see what works, you are finding out how to make shapes in fiction. Eventually you will know enough to be able to imagine the shape beforehand—sometimes before you even know what the story is going to be about.

You may have the impression that the forms of all short stories are pretty much alike, but that's not true. Since "form" in a story is really impossible to exhibit, I'm going to have to draw some diagrams and hope for the best.

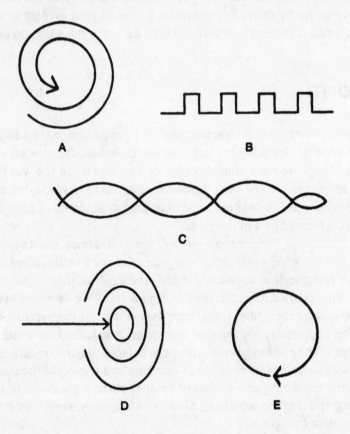

A, the spiral heading inward, is the story that begins far from its central mystery and approaches it by degrees. An example is my story "Masks," in which a succession of viewpoint characters is used, each one a little nearer, until finally we get to the central character and his secret is disclosed.

B, the straight course with a series of obstacles, is the classic "plot skeleton" story. "Rain," by W. Somerset Maugham, is an example. For reasons which I will show later, this form is rare in short fiction.

C is the story involving two characters or plot lines that keep intersecting and diverging until they meet at the end. This form is more common in novels than in short fiction; an example is Anthony Powell's *A Dance to the Music of Time.*

D is the story with the obvious and inevitable ending; an example is Isaac Asimov's "Nightfall."

E is a circular story; at the end, we see that we are back at the beginning—the characters are caught in a pattern and will never get out of it. An example is *Heaven's My Destination,* by Thornton Wilder.

These are some of the most familiar story forms, but there are all kinds of combinations and variants, some of which we will discuss later.

Story as Mechanism

Every story is a machine designed to evoke an organized series of responses in the reader. When the writer is clumsy, the mechanism shows (and we say in disappointment, "How mechanical!"). In a good story it is concealed and we are not aware of it, but it is there just the same, and every part of it has its function. The opening, for instance, arouses the reader's interest and curiosity; the next section involves him in the emotions and personalities of the characters, presents a problem to be solved or a mystery to be investigated, etc. The following section raises the reader's excitement or anticipation to a peak and then relieves it by revealing the resolution of the problem, the explanation of the mystery, or whatever.

These are the major parts of the mechanism, but there are others that are also essential. At every point, for instance, where a character acts in an unusual way, we must have something to show that her action is plausible.

In a story by a student of mine, a countryman takes his young son to the city for the first time. The father is determined to keep his son from being corrupted by the wicked city. A buyer they visit offers to keep the boy for a few weeks and teach him a little about the business. When the father refuses, the buyer becomes agitated and they quarrel. The boy says he wants to stay; the father reluctantly agrees.

I told the author there was a part missing. The buyer should be a *relative,* not just a business acquaintance; otherwise why does he insist so emotionally on taking in a boy he has just met? And why does the father consent? Without this piece, the story fails, just like any mechanism in which a necessary part has been left out.

To make these points clearer, I offer you here an annotated story of my own.

An Annotated Story: "Semper Fi"

There was a brisk little wind up here, flipping the white silk of his trousers
like flags against his body, ruffling his hair. Two thousand feet down past
the dangling tips of his shoes, he could see the mountains spread out, wave
after brilliant green wave. The palace was only a hollow square of ivory,
tiny enough to squash between thumb and forefinger. He closed his eyes,
drank the air with his body, feeling alive all the way to the tips of his fingers and toes.

He yawned, stretched with pleasure. It was good to get up here sometimes, away from all that marble and red velvet, the fountains, the girls in
their gauzy pants . . . There was something about this floating, this complete solitude and peace.

An insect voice said apologetically, "Pardon me, sir."

He opened his eyes, looked around. There it was, the one he called the
"bug footman," three inches of slender body, a face half human, half insect, wings a blur—flying as hard as it could to stay in one place.

"You're early," he said.

"No, sir. It's time for your therapy."

"That's all I hear from you—time for therapy."

"It's good for you, sir."

"Well, no doubt you're right."

"I'm sure I'm right, sir."

"Okay. Get lost."

The creature made a face at him, then veered away on the wind and diminished to a drifting speck of light. Gary Mitchell watched it until it was
lost against the sunlit green background. Then he tilted lazily in the air,
closed his eyes, and waited for the change.

He knew to the second when it would happen. "Bing," he said lazily,
and felt the world contract suddenly around him. The wind was gone;
mountains and sky were gone. He was breathing a more lifeless air. Even
the darkness behind his eyelids was a different color.

He moved cautiously, feeling the padded couch under him. He opened
his eyes. There was the same old room, looking so tiny and quaint that he
snorted with amusement. It was always the same, no matter how often he
came back to it. That struck him so funny that he rolled over, closing his
eyes again, shaken with silent laughter.

After a minute he lay back, emptying his lungs with a grunt, then breathing deeply through his nostrils. He felt good, even though his body ached a
little. He sat up and stared at the backs of his hands with amused affection.
Same old hands!

He yawned hard enough to crack the cartilage in his jaw, then grinned
and heaved himself up out of the hollow half-egg-shape of the couch.

This story is about a wish-fulfillment fantasy, and in the opening paragraph we are in the middle of it. If the reader has ever had such a fantasy, this opening will serve its purpose of drawing him in, arousing his curiosity (how can this man float two thousand feet in the air?), and giving him the first of a string of pleasures.

I want to imply the erotic elements of the fantasy rather than make them explicit, and that's why I don't show you Mitchell down there in the palace, among all his girls in their gauzy pants; having him float in midair is a convenient way of avoiding this, and at the same time it suggests what the story is about. (In the Freudian system, dreams of flying are sexual.)

Notice also that by the third paragraph something has begun to happen.

The bug footman confirms that this is a fantasy world. There are two allusions here to the works of Lewis Carroll—the frog footman in Alice in Wonderland, *and the Red Queen's remark to Alice, in* Through the Looking-Glass, *"Now* here, *you see, it takes all the running* you *can do, to keep in the same place."*

Should I have explained all this in the story, for the benefit of readers who have never read Alice *or have forgotten it? I don't think so. Readers who do recognize the allusions will get a pleasure that would have been spoiled by explaining it, and the others won't notice. (But beware of writing anything that will not make any sense at all unless the reader recognizes some esoteric allusion.)*

Although at this point the reader doesn't know exactly what's happening, I hope it will seem plausible in retrospect that the central character would invent some such device as this to prepare him for his return to the real world.

Mitchell is a little bit like someone coming down from an LSD experience—the same amusement at the drabness of reality, the same rather disturbing euphoria.

Notice also how much sensory detail you are getting in this and the following paragraphs. I'm trying to surround you with the story—make you feel that you are in it.

Here for the first time we see the machine that is responsible for all this. The machine is shaped like half an egg for a good reason: the designers didn't want it to look like a coffin.

Wires and tubing trailed from him in all directions. He pulled the cap off his head, breaking it free of the tiny plastic sockets in his skull. He dropped it, let it swing at the end of its cable. He unfastened the monitoring instruments from his chest, pulled off the rest of his gear, and strode naked across the room.

There was a click from the master clock on the control board, and Mitchell heard the water begin to hiss in the bathroom. "Suppose I don't want a shower?" he asked the clock. But he did; all according to routine.

He rubbed his palm over the stubble on his cheeks. Maybe he really should try to work out a gadget that would shave him while he was under the wire. A housing fitted to the lower part of his face, feedback to regulate the pressure . . . But the damned thing might be more trouble than it was worth.

Staring at himself in the mirror, he saw a glint of delighted irony come into his eyes. Same old thoughts! He got out the razor and began to shave.

The clock ticked again as he came from the bathroom, and a tray slid out of the conveyor onto the breakfast table. Scrambled eggs, bacon, orange juice, coffee. Mitchell went to the closet, took out pale-blue slacks and shirt, dressed, then sat down and ate, taking his time. The food was food—nourishment; that was about all you could say.

When he was done, he lit a cigarette and sat with half-closed eyes, letting the smoke spurt in two streams from his nostrils. Vague images drifted through his mind; he did not try to capture them.

The cigarette was a stub. He sighed, put it out. As he walked to the door, it seemed to him that the couch and the control panel were staring at him reproachfully. There was something abandoned and pathetic in the empty egg-shape, the scattered wires. "Tonight," he promised it. He opened the door and stepped through.

Pale, yellow-tinged sunlight came from the big picture window overlooking the East River. The philodendron in the ceramic pot had unfurled another leaf. On the wall across from the window hung an enormous abstraction by Pollock, upside down. Mitchell gave it an ironic grin.

Reports in their orange plastic binders were piled on one side of the long mahogany desk, letters on the other. In the center, on the green blotter, lay a block of soft pine and an open jackknife.

The red light of the intercom was blinking steadily. Mitchell sat down and looked at it for a moment, then touched the button. "Yes, Miss Curtis?"

"Mr. Price wants to know when you'll be available. Shall I tell him to come in?"

"Okay."

Mitchell picked up the top report, glanced at the sketches and diagrams inside, put it down again. He swiveled his chair around, leaned back and

This is here for plausibility and pleasure: plausibility, because Mitchell has an inventor's mind and would naturally think of things like this, and pleasure, because imaginary engineering is fun for many science-fiction readers.

Plausibility. This story takes place in the future; we have to be able to see that some things are different besides *the one invention that is the subject of the story.*

This reinforces Mitchell's amused superiority toward the real world, and it also tells us something about him by showing us the place where he works.

Again, something is about to happen; the reader is reassured that she is not going to have to wade through another three pages of description.

gazed sleepily out over the haze-yellowed landscape. A tug was moving slowly up the river, trailing puffs of yellow-white smoke. On the Queens side, housing units stood like a child's building blocks; sunlight glinted from the tiny rows of windows.

Curious to see all that still here, still growing; on the other side, he had leveled it years ago, filled it in with jungle. There was something quaint about it now, like an old yellowed snapshot. That was a little disturbing: coming back like this was always like re-entering the past. A faint sense of wrongness . . .

He heard the door click, and turned to see Jim Price with his hand on the knob. Mitchell grinned, waved a hand. "Hello, boy—good to see you. Knock 'em dead in Washington?"

"Not exactly." Price came forward with his heron's gait, folded himself into a chair, twitched, knotted his thin fingers together.

"Too bad. How's Marge?"

"Fine. I didn't see her last night, but she called in this morning. She asked me to ask you—"

"Kids all right?"

"Sure." Price's thin lips compressed; his brown eyes stared earnestly at Mitchell. He still seemed about twenty years old; to look at him, he had not changed since the days when Mitchell-Price, Inc., was an idea and a back room in Westbury. Only the clothes were different—the thousand-dollar suit, the perfectly knotted tie. And the fingernails; once they had been bitten to the quick, now they were manicured and shiny. "Mitch, let's get down to it. How is that deep probe gadget coming?"

"Got Stevenson's report on my desk—haven't looked through it yet."

Price blinked, shook his head. "You realize that project has been dragging on thirty-six months?"

"There's time," Mitchell said lazily. He reached for the knife and the block of wood.

"That's not the way you talked fifteen years ago."

"I was an eager beaver then," Mitchell said. He turned the block in his hands, feeling the little dusty burrs along the unfinished side. He set the blade against one edge, curled off the first long, sensuous shaving.

"Mitch, damn it, I'm worried about you—the way you've changed the last few years. You're letting the business slide."

"Anything wrong with the earnings reports?" Mitchell felt the cut surface with his thumb, turning to gaze out the window. It would be fun, he thought absently, to drift out into that hazy blue sky, over the tops of the toy buildings, still farther out, over the empty ocean. . . .

"We're making money, sure," Price's thin voice said impatiently. "On the mentigraph and the randomizer, one or two other little things. But we haven't put anything new on the market for five years, Mitch. What are we

Returning to Mitchell's perception of the real world as a drab, uninteresting place, this time with a stronger hint that using the machine has done something abnormal to his mind.

Price is a contrast to Mitchell in nearly every way. Playing them off against each other makes it easy for me to tell you more about each of them than I could if they were more alike—if Price were a dreamy pleasure-seeker, or Mitchell a dedicated organization man. Price is important also because his motives for promoting the machine are entirely different from Mitchell's.

Another suggestion that the machine has had an undesirable effect on Mitchell.

Their conversation is brief and elliptic because they know each other well and because they have had this conversation, in other forms, many times. They are talking to each other, not to the reader.

Earlier hints that Price is worried about Mitchell's mental state are made explicit here.

supposed to do, just coast? Is that all you want?"

Mitchell turned to look at his partner. "Good old Jim," he said affectionately. "When are you ever going to loosen up?"

The door clicked open and a dark-haired girl stepped in—Lois Bainbridge, Price's secretary. "Mr. Price, sorry to interrupt, but Dolly couldn't get you on the intercom."

Price glanced at Mitchell. "Push the wrong button again?"

Mitchell looked at the intercom with mild surprise. "Guess I did."

"Anyway," the girl said, "Mr. Diedrich is here, and you told me to tell you the minute—"

"Hell," said Price, standing up. "Where is he, in reception?"

"No, Mr. Thorwald has taken him down to Lab One. He has his lawyer and his doctor with him."

"I know it," Price muttered, prying nervously into his pockets. "Where did I put those damn— Oh, here." He pulled out some notes scrawled in pencil on file cards. "Okay, look, Lois, you phone down and tell them I'll be right there."

"Yes, Mr. Price." She smiled, turned, and walked out. Mitchell's mild gaze followed her. Not a bad-looking girl, as they went. He remembered that he had brought her over to the other side, three or four years ago, but of course he had made a lot of changes—slimmer waist, firmer bust . . . He yawned.

Price asked abruptly, "Do you want to sit in?"

"Want me to?"

"I don't know, Mitch—do you give a damn?"

"Sure." Mitchell got up, draped an arm around the other man's shoulders. "Let's go."

They walked together down the busy corridor. "Listen," Price said, "how long since you've been out for dinner?"

"Don't know. Month or two."

"Well, come out tonight. Marge told me to bring you for sure."

Mitchell hesitated, then nodded. "All right, Jim, thanks."

Lab One was the showcase—all cedar veneer and potted plants, with the egg-shaped mentigraph couch prominently displayed, like a casket in a mortuary. There were half a dozen big illuminated color transparencies on a table behind the couch, to one side of the control board.

Heads turned as they walked in. Mitchell recognized Diedrich at once—a heavyset pink-and-blond man in his early forties. The ice-blue eyes stared at him. Mitchell realized with a shock that the man was even more impressive, more hypnotic than he seemed on television.

Thorwald, the lab chief, made the introductions while white-coated technicians hovered in the background. "The Reverend Diedrich—and Mr. Edmonds, his attorney—and of course you know Dr. Taubman, at least by reputation."

Again, something is about to happen. I call your attention to these moments because they are essential to keep the story from becoming static.

The file cards will reappear. If I didn't mention them here first, they might seem like an abrupt and arbitrary invention later.

I told you that the designers didn't want the machine to look like a coffin, but it does anyway.
The transparencies will be used later, too.

Diedrich is the antagonist, and this gives us a clue that he is about to make trouble.
By now we realize that to some degree Price shares Diedrich's attitude toward the machine, and yet he is taking Mitchell's side against Diedrich. This gives us a hint that the problem is morally ambiguous.

They shook hands. Diedrich said, "I hope you understand the terms on which I am here. I'm not looking for any compromise." The pale eyes were intent and earnest. "Your people put it to me that I could attack the mentigraph more effectively if I had actually experienced it. If nothing changes my mind, that's just what I intend to do."

"Yes, we understand that, of *course,* Mr. Diedrich," said Price. "We wouldn't have it any other way."

Diedrich looked curiously at Mitchell. "You're the inventor of this machine?"

Mitchell nodded. "A long time ago."

"Well, what do you think about the way it has turned out—its effect on the world?"

"I like it," said Mitchell.

Diedrich's face went expressionless; he glanced away.

"I was just showing Mr. Diedrich these mentigraph projections," Thorwald said hurriedly, pointing to the transparencies. Two were landscapes, weird things, all orange trees and brown grass; one was a city scene, and the fourth showed a hill, with three wooden crosses silhouetted against the sky. "Dan Shelton, the painter, did these. He's enthusiastic about it."

"You can actually photograph what goes on in the subject's mind?" Edmonds asked, raising his black eyebrows. "I was not aware of that."

"It's a new wrinkle," Price answered. "We hope to have it on the market in September."

"Well, gentlemen, if you're ready—" Thorwald said.

Diedrich appeared to brace himself. "All right. What do I do? Shall I take my jacket off?"

"No, just lie down here, if you will," Thorwald answered, pointing to the narrow operating table. "Loosen your tie if it will make you more comfortable."

Diedrich got up on the table, his face set. A technician came up behind him with a basket-shaped object made of curved, crisscrossing metal pieces. She adjusted it gently over Diedrich's skull, tightened the wing nuts until it fitted. She took careful measurements, adjusted the helmet again, then pushed eight plungers, one after the other.

Taubman was looking over her shoulder as she removed the helmet. At the roots of Diedrich's hair, eight tiny purple spots were visible.

"This is merely a harmless dye, Doctor," Thorwald said. "All we are doing here is to establish the sites for the electrodes."

"Yes, all right," said Taubman. "And you assure me that none of them is in the pleasure center?"

"Definitely not. You know there is legislation against it, Doctor."

The technician had moved up again. With a small pair of scissors she cut

Diedrich has his own compelling reasons for being here; I haven't just pushed him onstage because I need him. He is as deeply involved as any of the others; the story (or a story) could be written from his viewpoint, making him the central character.

Playing off Diedrich against Mitchell. Price is used to Mitchell's hedonism and indifference, but Diedrich isn't, and he's repelled. That gives us another way to look at Mitchell, and it tells us something about Diedrich at the same time.

More about the transparencies. They have to be there because the action will turn on them later, and also for reasons of logic and plausibility: every basic invention leads to further inventions.

That isn't exactly what happens, but Edmonds is a lawyer, not a scientist.

This technical detail is necessary to reassure the reader that I know what I'm talking about. I use it for dramatic purposes in order to keep from boring anybody with a lecture.

Plausibility. Laboratory rats with electrodes in their pleasure centers have pushed the lever to stimulate themselves, ignoring food and water, until they fell from exhaustion. If a device like the mentigraph were put on the market, there would certainly be legislation to keep this from happening to human beings.

tiny patches of hair from the purple-marked spots. She applied lather, then, with an even smaller razor, shaved the patches clean. Diedrich lay quietly; he winced at the touch of the cool lather, but otherwise did not change expression.

"That's all of that," Thorwald said. "Now, Reverend Diedrich, if you'll sit over here—"

Diedrich got up and walked to the chair Thorwald pointed out. Over it hung a glittering basketwork of metal, like a more complicated and more menacing version of the helmet the technician had used.

"Just a moment," Taubman said. He went over to examine the mechanism. He and Thorwald spoke in low voices for a moment, then Taubman nodded and stepped back. Diedrich sat down.

"This is the only sticky part," Thorwald said. "But it really doesn't hurt. Now let's just get your head in this clamp—"

Diedrich's face was pale. He stared straight ahead as a technician tightened the padded clamp, then lowered the basket-shaped instrument. Standing on a dais behind the chair, Thorwald himself carefully adjusted eight metal cylinders, centering each over one of the shaved purple patches on Diedrich's skull. "This will be just like a pinprick," he said. He pressed a button. Diedrich winced.

"Now tell me what sensations you feel," said Thorwald, turning to a control panel.

Diedrich blinked. "I saw a flash of light," he said.

"All right, next."

"That was a noise."

"Yes, and this?"

Diedrich looked surprised; his mouth worked for a moment. "Something sweet," he said.

"Good. How about this?"

Diedrich started. "I felt something touch my skin."

"All right. Next."

"Pew!" said Diedrich, trying to turn his face away. "A terrible smell."

"Sorry. How about this one?"

"I felt warm for a moment."

"Okay, now this."

Diedrich's right leg twitched. "It felt as if it were doubled up under me," he said.

"Right. One more."

Diedrich stiffened suddenly. "I felt—I don't know how to describe it. *Satisfied*." His cold eyes went from Mitchell to Thorwald. His jaw was set hard.

"Perfect!" Thorwald said, getting down from the platform. He was grinning with pleasure. Mitchell glanced at Price, saw him wiping his palms with a handkerchief.

Plausibility again. Every human brain is unique, as I told you; these tests are necessary to make sure the electrodes are in the right places. All this preliminary fussing around makes the scene more plausible in another way: the reader may have experienced similar things in hospital procedures, and will expect them here.

The eighth electrode, unlike the others, produces a change in the subject's emotional state.

The cylinders retracted; the technician unfastened the headclamp. "That's all of that," said Thorwald heartily. "You can step down."

Diedrich got out of the chair, his jaw still set. One hand went up to fumble at his skull.

"Pardon me," said Taubman. He parted Diedrich's hair with his fingers and stared at the little gray plastic button, almost flush with the scalp, that had covered one of the purple spots.

Mitchell drifted over to stand beside Price. "Our friend didn't like that jolt in number eight," he murmured. "Careful, boy."

"I know," Price answered in an undertone. Across the room, Thorwald and the technicians had seated Diedrich in another chair and put the cap on his head. One of the technicians began showing him big sheets of colored pasteboard, while another, a pale young man with big ears, read dials and punched keys at the control console.

"This is a pretty big gamble you're taking, son," Mitchell said. "You know if we just make him mad, he can really smear us. How'd you get so brave?"

Price scowled, shuffled his feet. "Don't bury me yet," he muttered.

A technician was passing vials of scent under Diedrich's nose, one after another.

"Something up your sleeve?" Mitchell asked; but he had lost interest, and did not hear Price's reply. The technicians were walking Diedrich up and down, getting him to bend, raise his arms, turn his head. When they finally let him sit down again, his face was slightly flushed. Mitchell was thinking dreamily that he could use Diedrich on the other side—make a Teutonic knight out of him, noble, humorless, and fierce. But reduce him to about half-size . . . that would be funny.

"We won't try to calibrate the emotional responses this time, Mr. Diedrich," Thorwald was saying. "That's more difficult and complicated—it takes quite a while. But you've got enough here to give you a very good idea of the device."

Diedrich put up a hand to feel the cap on his head, the cluster of wires emerging from the middle of it. "All right," he said grimly. "Go ahead."

Thorwald looked a little worried. He motioned to the technician at the console. "Input one, Jerry." To Diedrich he said, "Just close your eyes, if you will, and let your hands relax."

The man at the console touched a button. An expression of surprise crossed Diedrich's face. His right hand moved spasmodically, then lay still. A moment later he turned his head aside. His jaws made slow chewing motions. Then he opened his eyes.

"Amazing," he said. "A banana—I peeled it and then ate a bite. But—they weren't my hands."

"Yes, of course—that was a recording made by another subject.

By making these further tests, the technicians are able to calibrate the machine so that it can stimulate a specific smell or sight or kinesthetic sensation or whatever.

These repeated daydreams of Mitchell's, brief as they are, show that his attitudes toward his fantasy world carry over into reality.

However, when you learn to use the other circuits, Mr. Diedrich, you can run that through again and change it until they *are* your hands—or make any other changes you like."

Diedrich's expression showed controlled distaste. He said, "I see." Watching him, Mitchell thought, *He's going to go home and write a speech that will blister our tails.*

"You'll see what I mean in just a moment," Thorwald was saying. "This time there won't be any primary recording—you'll do it all yourself. Just lean back, close your eyes, and imagine some picture, some scene—"

Diedrich fingered his watch impatiently. "You mean you want me to try to make a picture like those?" He nodded toward the transparencies ranged along the wall.

"No, no, nothing like that. We won't project it, and only you will see what it is. Just visualize a scene, and wherever it seems vague or out of proportion, keep on changing it and adding to it . . . Go ahead, try it."

Diedrich leaned back, closed his eyes. Thorwald nodded to the man at the console.

Price moved abruptly away from Mitchell, strode over to the chair. "Here is something that may help you, Mr. Diedrich," he said, bending close. He looked at the notes in his hand, and read aloud, "And it was about the sixth hour, and there was a darkness over all the earth until the ninth hour. And the sun was darkened, and the veil of the temple was rent in the midst."

Diedrich frowned; then his face relaxed. There was a long silence. Diedrich began to frown again. After a moment his hands moved spasmodically on the arms of the chair. His jaw muscles lost their tightness; his chin dropped slightly. After another moment he began breathing quickly and shallowly, lips parted.

Taubman stepped over, frowning, and attempted to take his pulse, but Diedrich knocked his hand away. Taubman glanced at Price, who shook his head and put a finger to his lips.

Diedrich's face had turned into a mask of grief. Moisture appeared under his closed eyelids, began to run down his cheeks. Watching him closely, Price nodded to Thorwald, who turned toward the console and made a chopping motion.

Diedrich's tear-filled eyes slowly opened.

"What was it, Mr. Diedrich?" Edmonds asked, bending toward him. "What happened?"

Diedrich's voice was low and hoarse. "I saw—I saw—" His face contorted and he began to sob. He bent over as if in pain, hands clasped so tightly that the fingers turned red and yellow-white in patches.

Price turned away, took Mitchell by the arm. "Let's get out of here," he

This explains how the machine enables Mitchell to create his own fantasy world and manipulate it as he chooses.

Now we begin to see that the file cards and the transparencies are a trap for Diedrich.

Giving Taubman something plausible to do, just to remind the reader that he is here.

A bit part for Edmonds, too. If there isn't anything for these people to do, they shouldn't be here.

muttered. In the corridor, he began to whistle.

"Think you're pretty slick, don't you, boy?" Mitchell asked.

Price's grin made him look like a mischievous small boy. "I know I am, old buddy," he said.

There were four of them at dinner—Price and his good-looking red-haired wife; Mitchell, and a girl he had never met before. Her name was Eileen Novotny; she was slender, gray-eyed, quiet. She was divorced, Mitchell gathered, and had a small daughter.

After dinner they played a rubber of bridge. Eileen was a good player, better than Mitchell; but when he blundered, once or twice, she only gave him a glance of ironic commiseration. She did not talk much; her voice was low and well modulated, and Mitchell found himself waiting for her to speak again.

When the rubber was over, she stood up. "I'm glad to have met you, Mitch," she said, and gave him her warm hand for a moment. "Thank you for a lovely dinner and a nice evening," she said to Marge Price.

"You're not going already?"

"Afraid I have to—my sitter can only stay till ten, and it will take me a good hour to get up to Washington Heights."

She paused at the door, glancing back at Mitchell. He could well imagine how it might be with this girl—the long walks, the intimate little restaurants, holding hands, the first kiss . . . Price and his wife were looking at him expectantly.

"Good night, Eileen," he said.

After she was gone, Marge brought in some beer and excused herself. Price settled himself in a relaxer and lit a pipe. Squinting at Mitchell over the bowl, he said mildly, "You might have given the girl a taxi-ride home, old buddy."

"And start all over again? No thanks, old buddy—I've had it."

Price flipped out his match, dropped it into an ashtray. "Well, it's your life."

"So I've always imagined."

Price shifted uncomfortably in the chair. "So I'm a matchmaker," he said, scowling. "Dammit, I don't like to see what's happening to you. You spend more time under the wire than out of it. It isn't healthy, it isn't good for you."

Mitchell grinned and held out a hand. "Indian rassle?"

Price flushed. "All right, all right, I know you work out at the gym every week—you're in good shape physically. That's not what I'm talking about, and you know it damn well."

Mitchell took a long pull at his can of beer. It was lighter and maltier than he liked, but it was cold, at least, and felt good going down his throat.

Part of the moral ambiguity, to which we will return later. Mitchell thinks the machine is harmless; Price doesn't. Which of them is more irresponsible?

This is Mitchell's chance, probably his last one, to give up his fantasy life and return to the real world. The choice is implicit in the story, but this scene makes it actual. The "hinge" of the story is here.

The hand is warm because Mitchell's is cool: that tells us something about both of them.

A hint about Mitchell's past: he has been married, but isn't now.

If Mitchell were in poor shape physically, it would be too easy to say that the mentigraph is bad for him.

What about a green beer for St. Paddy's day? Give it a suggestion of mint—just a touch . . .

"Say something," Price said.

Mitchell's eyes focused on him slowly. "Hmm. Think Diedrich will stop being a nuisance now?"

Price made a sour face. "Okay, change the subject. Sure, I think Diedrich will stop being a nuisance. We're sending him a complete rig—couch, control board, library of crystals. And he'll take it. He's hooked."

"Dirty trick?" Mitchell suggested.

"No, I don't think so."

"You planted that picture of the three crosses, didn't you? Then, just to make sure, you stepped up and read him a paragraph from the crucifixion scene in Matthew. Pretty foxy."

"Luke," said Price. "Yeah, pretty foxy."

"Tell me something," Mitchell said. "Just for curiosity—how long since you've been under the wire yourself?"

Price looked at his hand, clasped around the pipe-bowl. "Four years," he said.

"How come?"

"Don't like what it does to me." He folded his free hand around the one that held the pipe; his knuckles cracked, one after another.

"Made you twenty million," Mitchell said gently.

"You know I don't mean that." Price unclenched his hands, leaned forward. "Listen, the Pentagon turned down that contract for forty thousand training crystals. They decided they don't like what it does to people, either."

"Keeps them from being eager little beavers," Mitchell said. "My back aches for the Pentagon."

"What about the contract—does your back ache for that?"

"You know, James, I don't understand you," Mitchell said. "One minute you're telling me the mentigraph is worse than hashish, heroin, booze, and adultery, all put together. The next, you're complaining because we don't sell more of 'em. How do you explain that?"

Price did not smile. "Let's say I'm a worrywart. You know I keep talking about pulling out—maybe I'll do it some day—but till I do, I'm responsible to the corporation and I'll do my best for it. That's business. When I worry about you, it's friendship."

"I know it, old buddy."

"Maybe I worry about the whole world once in a while, too," Price said. "What's going to happen when everybody's got a private dream-world? Where's the old Colonial spirit then?"

Mitchell snorted. "Have you ever done any reading about Colonial times? I did some research on it years ago. They used to drink a horrible

Tying up the plotline about Price's trap for Diedrich, just to make sure the reader isn't left wondering what happened.

Another touch of ambiguity: if the Pentagon doesn't like the machine, can it be all bad?

"That's business." I have great sympathy for both these people, but I must say I admire Mitchell more.

thing called flip, made out of rum and hard cider, and they'd plunge a hot poker into it to make it froth up. You could tell the drunkards just by seeing who had an apple orchard."

Price swung his legs off the relaxer, put his elbows on his knees. "All right, what about this? You've got it made, haven't you—you can spend half your time in a world where everything is just the way you like it. You don't need that sweet kid that walked out of here half an hour ago—you've got twenty better-looking than her. And they're on call any time. So why get married, why raise a family? Just tell me this—what's going to happen to the world if the brightest guys in it drop out of the baby-making business? What happens to the next generation?"

"I can answer that one too."

"Well?"

Mitchell lifted his beer can in salute, staring at Price over the shiny top. "The hell with them," he said.

Revisionist history. I love this kind of thing, and will sneak it into a story any chance I get. It isn't essential here, but it strengthens Mitchell's argument (the Colonial Americans were out for pleasure, too).

Or, "What did posterity ever do for me?" At this point, I want to leave you thinking, Is Mitchell wrong? And if so, why?

Some years ago I published an annotated version of another story, "Masks," in a volume called *Those Who Can,* edited by Robin Scott Wilson. Shortly after it appeared I had a visit from a young writer, and he asked me, with a disbelieving wrinkle in his brow, "Did you really put all that stuff in there on purpose?" I answered yes, but I realized much later that what he really wanted to know was, "Did you put all that stuff in deliberately and consciously?" Of course I didn't. But I was aware of it in the back of my mind, and sometimes (partly) in the front. I know how a story feels when its mechanism is working, and I can tell when it stops working: then I try this and that until it works again. Looking back, later, I can analyze the mechanism in detail—not while I'm writing.

What I want you to do is not to learn this complicated art all at once, but just to become aware that at every point a story should be producing *some* response in the reader.

The best way to learn how this is done is to read fiction critically, asking yourself whenever you feel some response to the story, "How did she do that? Why did she do this?" Begin with stories of the kind that you ordinarily read for pleasure.

The best place to study technique is in the work of first-class genre novelists like John D. MacDonald, the author of the Travis McGee series. In these novels the technique is right up front (and it's very good technique); in the work of literary writers it is usually well concealed. When you have found out something about how the authors create their effects, you may find that your pleasure in these stories is a little diminished. That's all right. Now you can read more subtle and complex stories and be overcome by the same wonder: "How in the world did she do that?" And you'll keep on learning.

Often you may find that after half a page or so of a good story you will be swept away by the narrative (just as the author intended), forgetting all about your intention to read critically. If that happens, go back and read it again, and again, until the story is so familiar that it has lost some of its power over you, and you can examine the mechanism behind the mystery.

Structure

You know what the structure of a bridge is, because it is completely exposed, and you probably understand pretty well what the structure of your own skeleton is, even though it is entirely concealed. But what does "structure" in a story mean?

Structure means the combination and arrangement of parts to make a functioning whole. But before you can distinguish between good and bad structure, you have to know what the device is *for*. A bridge has to bear a certain load, including its own weight; a good bridge design, therefore, is one that will carry the load (including a margin for safety) with the least structural weight. Your skeleton must support and articulate your body, again with the least structural weight.

Structure in a story is the framework that holds it together. I don't mean plot—we'll get to that later. You can look at two stories and see that their structure is similar, even when their plots are different. Each may begin with a group of people waiting for someone else to arrive, for instance, producing a feeling of anticipation and foreboding; then there may be a middle section in which the newcomer comes into conflict with the others somehow, then a section in which the conflict is resolved and some final revelation is made. This very general outline would describe Noel Coward's play *Blithe Spirit* and Willa Cather's story "The Sculptor's Funeral" about equally well. Their plots have nothing to do with each other; in fact, Cather's story has very little plot.

In the opening of *Blithe Spirit* a novelist and his wife are waiting for the arrival of two guests and a medium named Madam Arcati; the novelist wants to observe her technique for use in a book he is about to write. (How I wish we had that book!) In "The Sculptor's Funeral" the residents of a small Kansas town are waiting for the corpse of a famous sculptor to arrive on the train. But it's the same structure: first the short introductory part, then the middle section whose conflict creates rising tension, then the conclusion:

(Looks like a bridge, doesn't it?)

In both these stories the setting, the characters, the emotion, and the situation are all closely linked; there is no part of the story that is arbitrary or irrelevant. That makes it strong. Parts of a story that are not structurally connected to other parts are like dangling bits of a piece of furniture; they just get in the way. This is what C. S. Lewis meant when he said, "Whatever in a work of art is not used, is doing harm."

Good structure in a story can be appreciated for its own sake, just as it can in a bridge. What it is for, however, is to draw the reader into the story, keep her reading, and satisfy her at the end. Notice how the tension rises in the introductory section, rises again in the middle section, then falls in the final section when the conflict is resolved, the mystery explained, or whatever. If tension falls to zero anywhere in the story before the end, the story will probably be a failure.

Suppose, for instance, that your story begins with a scientist in a government laboratory who is trying to develop a vaccine for a new and dangerous strain of pneumonia. The work is routine and not very promising. After three pages of this, the central character leaves for a weekend and goes to see her father, who, it turns out, is ill with the new disease. The daughter gets him into a hospital, works night and day on the vaccine, and perfects it in time to save her father's life.

Here we have a structure that looks like this:

After the first little peak, the tension in the story falls to zero. Nothing is happening or about to happen in the laboratory; the central character is off to see her father, whom the reader has not met and has no reason to care about.

The first section should be amputated: the story should begin with the central character's visit to her father.

The corollary to C. S. Lewis's statement, quoted above, is that anything that *is* used, anything that connects two or more parts of a story, strengthens it. To illustrate this, here are some of the things that are used in "Semper Fi":

	Pages
Mitchell's fantasy experiences	62, 66, 68, 74, 80
His attitude toward the real world	62, 64, 66, 78, 82
The "mentigraph"	62, 66, 68, 70, 72, 74
The file cards	68, 74, 76, 80
Price's dinner invitation	68, 78
The transparencies	68, 70, 76, 80

If we represent the page numbers by numbered dots in a row, and draw arcs between them to show the connections, then the first item, Mitchell's fantasy experiences, will look like this:

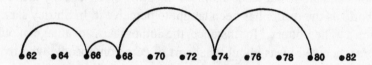

If we now do the same thing for each of the other items, and plot them on the same chart, it comes out looking like this. (The first three items are plotted above the line and the last three below, just to keep the arcs from getting in each other's way.)

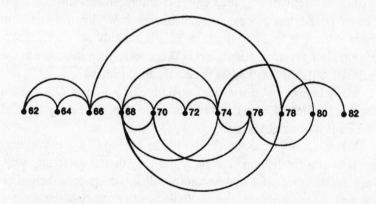

This chart is an attempt to make visible the relationships that exist in any well-structured story. (It demonstrates, incidentally, that the story has a clearly defined beginning, middle, and end.)

Again I have to remind you that I didn't draw any such diagram when I was writing the story; I just knew, for example, that if Mitchell was going to go to Price's apartment for dinner in the final section, he ought to be invited earlier. Don't try to draw charts like this one for your stories before you write them, unless you just like to play with charts. Do study this one to become aware of the many ways in which parts of a story can be connected.

I have been talking about structure before discussing plot, because I want to make sure you understand that they are not interchangeable terms. "Plot" is one way of organizing a story. There are many other ways. For example, there are what Kate Wilhelm calls "lean-to" stories, in which the structure built by the author does not stand alone but leans against something else—usually the real world as the reader has been taught to perceive it. In Shirley Jackson's "The Lottery," for instance, the author takes advantage of our preconceived ideas about what sort of ceremony people who live in a village might be gathering to perform on a pleasant spring day. This is the structure against which the story leans. The story has no structure of its own except for the ceremony itself; that's enough.

The physical movement of a story—just moving your character from one place to another—can provide a structure. Notice how this is done in "Semper Fi": the central character moves through a series of connected places, in each of which we learn something more about him and his situation. This is a highly economical way of organizing a story, because it builds a satisfying structure at the same time that it establishes necessary background.

Many beginners' stories lack structure of any kind. One reason for this has been ferreted out by a student of mine, Sandy Beadle. She calls it "tunnel vision."

When you think about a story you are going to write, you may see it as a bright disk up in front, with a gray tunnel stretching away into the distance, and maybe another disk, not quite so bright, at the end. That's because you are looking at the story-to-be-written the way you see a story when you read it. You're looking down the tunnel of the story, and of course you can't see its structure very clearly. To see structure in a story, you must look at it from the side.

In their answers to a questionnaire I handed out at the 1984 Clarion Writers' Workshop, most students said they begin writing a story when they have a general idea and a beginning—they work out the rest as they go along, and hope to wind up with some sort of ending. This is the tunnel-vision method. If you are writing this way, and it isn't working, try these methods of turning the tunnel on its side.

1. Do you begin with one vivid image? Look for another one at the end of the story. Now at least you have both ends, and maybe that's enough. If it isn't, look for at least one other image in the middle. Remember that in the universe of your story, you are God. You have the magic power to spy on your characters wherever they are. Not to use this power is to deny yourself one of the great forbidden pleasures.

2. Whenever you have one of these vivid images in your mind, *look around.* What do you see? What books are on the shelves, what kind of carpet on the floor? What do you see when you look out the window?

3. Who else is in the room, or in the room next door? Who are the other people who are important to your character? Which ones does she love or hate? How do they feel about her?

4. *Look back* into the past of your character. What experiences has she had that will influence the way she behaves now? What *secret* does she have that she has never told anyone?

5. Ask yourself, what does the story mean? If it doesn't mean anything, you probably have not thought about it deeply enough. When you do have a sense of what the story means to you, ask yourself, does the ending support that meaning? If not, you know you need a different ending.

By going back and forth along the tunnel of the story before you write it, you will find you are able to make all the parts fit together. In a well-constructed story, every part fits; the ending is implicit in the beginning. You may be able to bring this off by a kind of unconscious juggling act as you write, but it is much safer to plan it in advance.

The Natural Series and the Dramatic Series

A true story, or one taken as true, doesn't need embellishment and it doesn't need artistic interpretation. Its truth gives it an intrinsic interest, and that's enough.

Fiction, on the other hand, is offered as an invention—a lie. The fiction writer's task is not to tell the literal truth, but to lie artfully—to lie so well that the reader's interest is engaged as if he were reading the truth.

Fiction involves two kinds of events, the natural and the dramatic series. The natural series of events is composed of things like getting up in the morning, eating breakfast, going to work, talking to friends on the phone, reading the mail, shopping for dinner, etc. Events like these are necessary in fiction to give an illusion of reality and to fill the pauses between dramatic events. (Even in a play, where the action is severely limited, people light cigarettes, turn on the stereo, brush their hair, and so on.)

The dramatic series is made up of those events, and only those, that form a connected and meaningful story. Real life does not often furnish a dramatic series; if it did, our instinct for order and design would be satisfied, and very likely we would feel no need for fiction.

It is a common mistake to set out to write a series of natural events in the hope that it will somehow turn itself into a dramatic series. Natural events have no innate disposition to do this, and such a story can prolong itself indefinitely, like toothpaste being squeezed out of a tube, until even the author sees it is hopeless and gives up.

Coincidences are a normal part of the natural series of events, but as a rule they should not be made part of the dramatic series. (The heroine's lover should not just happen to wander into the woods and stumble across the lonely cabin in which she is about to be raped by the villain, for instance.) The dramatic events of your story should be reasonably plausible. Real events have no such restriction, and that's why the truth is no excuse. Your story may be based on a real incident, and it may have happened just as you told it, and it may be implausible just the same.

Situation

A situation is a slice of the story; the opening situation is where the narrative begins. A dramatic situation is unstable—you know it can't stay this way forever—and it has at least two possible outcomes, one very desirable and one not.

In a plotted story, the opening situation should always contain the germ of conflict. For example, a wife is pretending to be content with her subordinate role in her marriage although she is deeply dissatisfied. This is her situation; but you can see how inevitably and strongly it leads to conflict.

C. S. Forester, the author of the Horatio Hornblower novels, once observed that there are two kinds of writers: those who invent a character and then look for something for him to do, and those who invent a situation and then look for a character to put in it.

If you begin with a situation, what you want is a character who has a stake in how the story turns out. (James Blish's device for extracting character from situation was to ask himself, "Who does this hurt?")

In an unplotted story or a circular story, the situation at the end may be the same as the one at the beginning, but the reader understands it better at the end than she did at first. In other stories, the two situations are usually different in some important way. The progression from one situation to the other is what makes the story. The *difference* between the two is what makes drama. (For example, the scullery maid who becomes a duchess, or the overconfident traveler who dies trying to light a fire.)

An Exercise in Situation

Choose three published plotted stories that you like, and for each one write a one-sentence description of the situation (a) at the beginning of the story and (b) at the end.

Now you can see that the author's problem was how to get from *a* to *b*. Look again at each story to see how she did it. How many intermediate situations does the story pass through? How many times does something unexpected happen? List these, and compare them with a similar list made from one of your own stories. Do you see the difference? Are your stories *too simple*?

Conflict

A characteristic of all living organisms, including people, goldfish, and blades of grass, is a drive to achieve homeostasis or equilibrium. You see this in temperature control, for instance—when you are too cold, you shiver; when you are too hot, you sweat. (Or you adjust the thermostat, or change your clothes.) Every living thing is constantly trying to balance its internal needs against the pressures of the environment—and "environment" includes the other members of its own species. Think of a family of four people, for example. Each member is trying to reach some accommodation with the other three; it isn't always easy. When the demands of one person rise to a level that another person can't tolerate, there is conflict.

Conflict is something pushing back. If your character wants to get from here to there, and nothing is pushing back, there is no conflict. Or if your character is ground down by circumstances, and *she* isn't pushing back, there is no conflict.

Conflict doesn't necessarily involve physical assault or even shouting matches. Don't confuse conflict and confrontation. Confrontation may be the expression of a conflict (as in the film *High Noon*), but it may express nothing more than irritation or petulance. Even when confrontation leads to violence, it still may not express a true conflict. Too many young writers (almost all male) fill their stories with empty violence—bullets and gobbets of flesh flying in all directions—as a substitute for meaningful action. Violence denatures itself very rapidly. It should be used sparingly and for maximum effect; it should never be used when the story does not demand it.

Sometimes what is pushing back is just the difficulty of a puzzle, or the mystery of a situation, or the necessity of a hard choice. As different as they are, all these types of stories have one thing in common—they are *difficult* for the central character.

Don't Make It Easy

Among the endless temptations for a writer to be lazy or self-indulgent, wish-fulfillment fantasies are especially dangerous. You think, How nice it would be if some deserving person could have an amulet that would give her good luck all her life! So you begin the story: Your heroine finds the amulet, and thereafter a series of nice things happens. A taxi pulls up just when she needs it, someone gives her tickets to a play, where she meets a kind, gentle, handsome man who happens to be a veterinarian and cures her cat, and so on. Here are all sorts of incidents, but what has become of the story? There is none, because there is no conflict, no difficulty, no tension.

When you start with an idea that makes you say, "Wouldn't this be wonderful?" ask yourself, "What's the catch?" Then it may generate a story. (And there's always a catch.)

Our interest is aroused when a character's freedom of action is limited, either by forces outside himself or by obsession. A driven or obsessed character can't shrug and walk away from the situation; he has to play the game out to the end, and because we know that, we are willing to stay and see him do it. There would not be many paying customers for football games if the players could decide it was really too boring to finish the game that day.

I think there are two or three different reasons why stories about obsessed or driven characters are so powerful. Most of us are so fragmented in our desires and hopes for the future that it's a relief to be, for a while, someone who knows exactly what she wants and is willing to do anything to get it. Another reason is that such stories give us a strong sense of danger; we know that the obsessed character's extraordinary behavior is bound to get her into trouble eventually, and we wait for it to happen. And a third reason, maybe, is that characters like this exhibit the sin of hubris, overweening pride, the basis of classical tragedy. They are arrogantly attempting to impose their will on the universe, and we subconsciously expect them to be struck down. They are like people walking a high wire, twenty stories up, without a net; we stand below, waiting to see them fall.

Sometimes a writer has difficulty getting conflict into her stories because she likes her characters too well to want to hurt them and has a distaste for violence. If you are such a writer, think of the pressures you are under

- to produce at work or in school
- to make money, if you support a family
- to protect small children

If any one of these pressures suddenly becomes more acute, you are vividly aware of it—you feel anguish or even despair, but you gather your strength to fight back—probably not with physical violence, but you will find some way. That's conflict. What happens *next* is the story.

Which of two elevators will you take to get down from the fiftieth floor? That's a trivial decision—but suppose you knew in advance that only one would get you to the lobby alive? Life-and-death problems engage our attention because the survival instinct is so strong. But "life" may mean different things to different people. To some, the loss of honor, self-respect, or the respect of peers may be the same as the loss of life. You don't need to have the hero of every story hanging over the edge of a building; you can arouse his survival instinct in more subtle ways.

Please note that except in detective stories and some other kinds of category fiction, professional problems don't make stories in themselves—spies spying, lawyers lawyering, plumbers plumbing. You may begin with a professional problem, but it had better turn pretty quickly into a personal one. In my story "Four in One," for example, a biologist is studying a strange organism on an alien planet. That's a professional problem—until he falls into it. Now he's still studying the organism—from the inside—but it's a personal problem, because he's got to understand the organism if he wants to survive.

Plot

You know this story, but in case you have forgotten: A man in a rooming house was in the habit of taking off his shoes at night and dropping them on the floor one at a time, with a pause for rumination in between. The lodger below had complained about this many times. One night, after dropping the first shoe, the man suddenly remembered the complaints and put the second shoe down gently.

After twenty minutes had passed, an agonized wail came up from the room below: "For God's sake, drop the other shoe!"

In one way or another, every plotted story makes us wait for the other shoe to drop. We are waiting for the resolution of a conflict, or the solution to a puzzle, or the explanation of a mystery, or just the completion of a pattern, and it is this anticipation, as much as anything else, that makes us read on.

A plot, then, is a series of imaginary events designed to create anticipation at a high pitch, either in the form of anxiety (in a story of conflict or mystery), or of curiosity (in a puzzle story). If you can build such a series, you can plot.

In a plotted story, the ending may take the form of a resolution, a revelation, a decision, an explanation, or a solution.

Resolution is the end of a conflict by the victory of one side or the other. **Revelation** means the exposure of something previously hidden. In a **decision** story, the ending comes when the central character makes up her mind about something important and difficult. **Explanation,** obviously, provides the ending for a story about a mystery, and **solution** provides the ending for a puzzle.

The Story of Resolution

In order to discuss this, we must talk about an ideal structure that is seldom found in its complete form in short fiction. One name for it is the "plot skeleton." The skeleton has five bones:

1. a believable and sympathetic central character;
2. his urgent and difficult problem;

3. his attempts to resolve the problem, which fail and make his situation more desperate;

4. the crisis, his last chance to win;

5. the successful resolution, brought about by means of the central character's own courage, ingenuity, etc.

The reverse of this plot is the story in which the central character is the villain; the story ends with his defeat rather than with his victory.

"Rain," by W. Somerset Maugham, has a complete plot skeleton if you take Miss Thompson as the central character. Miss Thompson is a raucous prostitute, forced by a quarantine to stay over at Pago Pago on her way from Honolulu to Apia. Here the missionary, Mr. Davidson, threatens to make trouble for the governor unless he deports her to the mainland, where a prison sentence awaits her. Her problem is thus serious and urgent. She tries to solve it first by appealing to the governor and to Dr. Macphail. These attempts failing, she gives in to Davidson and allows him to save her soul. She becomes a changed woman, utterly crushed and transformed. Then she seduces Davidson, who cuts his throat in remorse and horror; the next day she is dressed and made up in her old manner, and her raucous laughter rings out again.

Some writing manuals insist that this is the only structure of successful popular fiction, but in fact, although many short stories begin this way, nearly all of them lack the third element (the failed attempts) and the fifth (the central character's victory by his own efforts). The third is left out because it is too hard to cram into a short story, and the fifth because repetition would make it dull. When a story has only two possible endings, it is hard to surprise the reader with either; when the story has only one conventional ending (the triumph of the hero), it is even harder.

Nevertheless, most plotted stories are built around some kind of conflict or competition whose outcome is in doubt. The beginning of the story sets forth the terms of the competition; the middle is the contest itself; the ending is the outcome. (Here's the bridge structure again.) If this were all there was to it, most plotted stories would be unbearably predictable. In practice, what usually happens is that the author uses the conflict structure to *misdirect* the reader—the real meaning of the story turns out to be something altogether different.

Conflict can be just a way of exposing character—we learn things about people when they are under stress that we would never find out otherwise. Aside from this, conflict is a convenient and simple way of keeping the reader interested until you can lead her to whatever it is that you want to reveal.

The Story of Revelation

Notice that even in Maugham's story, which has a complete plot skeleton, the ending is not narrated where it naturally falls but is brought out later with an air of revelation. More often, revelation *replaces* resolution. In Roald Dahl's "Man from the South," for example, the plot concerns a strange little man who offers to bet his new car against a young sailor's left little finger that the sailor's lighter won't light ten times in a row. He ties the sailor's hand to the table between them with the little finger extended, and waits with a cleaver poised while the sailor flicks his lighter. The sailor gets up to eight, and then the little man's wife comes in and stops the contest. He has no car to bet, she tells the onlookers; he has nothing, in fact, because she won it all from him long ago. She reaches for the car key on the table, and the others see that there is only a thumb and one finger on that hand.

Notice that either of the endings we are led to expect would be disappointing (the little man cuts off the sailor's finger, or the sailor gets into the car and drives away). The conflict with which the story begins is only a sham, a work of misdirection. What we are waiting for is the third ending, the surprising one.

In other stories, there is no pretense of a dramatic conflict—the revelation is all there is. An example is Shirley Jackson's "The Lottery," about an ancient ritual performed every year in a New England village. Lots are drawn, first by families, then by households, then by individuals, until one person, a woman, has been selected. This process occupies the whole of the story until the last few paragraphs. Only then, when the villagers begin to stone the woman to death, do we find out what the lottery has been about.

Notice that in this story, although there is no conflict at all in the usual sense, there is *rising tension* because the choice is continually being narrowed down, and also because we know that we are coming closer to the revelation of the meaning of the lottery. If you can create rising tension, it doesn't matter whether there's conflict or not.

Another example of rising tension in a story without a conventional plot is Joseph Conrad's "Youth," about a ship foundering in a storm, in which the old captain might be said to have a problem in the plot-skeleton sense, but the narrator has none—he has no power of choice at any point, except at the end, when he can decide to try to keep near the other boats or go off by himself. And yet it is the narrator who is the central figure, the one in whom we are intensely interested; the old captain is almost incidental.

Trick Endings

Very short stories with surprising endings are called trick-ending stories. William Sydney Porter ("O. Henry") wrote hundreds of these stories and made a career of them. An example is his story of the widowed bakery owner who begins to have romantic feelings about a rather shabby man who comes in every day to buy a loaf of stale bread. On an impulse, she cuts a loaf open and conceals a pat of butter in it to surprise him. He comes back later, in a rage: he is an architect who uses stale bread to erase pencil lines from his drawings, and she has just ruined six months' work.

Trick-ending stories are out of fashion among the critics, but editors still buy them. Nearly half of all mystery short stories fall into this category.

The Story of Decision

Stories of this kind usually concern divided interests or loyalties. In John Collier's "The Steel Cat," for instance, a man has invented a better mousetrap: the mouse walks out along a beam to get the bait, the beam tilts, the mouse falls into a jar of water and drowns. The inventor has been all over the country demonstrating the trap with the aid of a beloved pet mouse, but without success. In Chicago he shows the trap to a buyer who is impressed, but who becomes suspicious when the inventor tries to rescue his pet; he won't believe the trap works until he sees the mouse dead. The anguished inventor lets it drown.

A pitfall in the story of decision is that the choice that faces your character may appear too simple—whether to accept her lover's offer of marriage or stay home and be a poor relation, for instance. The reader may think the girl is a dolt for even hesitating—the ending will fail because it is obvious. The trick is to make the choice really difficult, and to keep the reader from knowing in advance what your character's decision will be.

The Story of Explanation

An example is Nathaniel Hawthorne's "My Kinsman, Major Molineux," in which a young man from the country is sent to a colonial New England town to seek his fortune with his relative, Major Molineux, an officer of the Crown. He receives strange answers wherever he inquires for his relative; men in curious garments are abroad on the streets with their faces painted. One of these tells the young man, "Watch here an hour, and Major Molineux will pass by." At length a noisy torchlit procession appears; in the midst of it is Major Molineux, in an open cart, tarred and feathered. The mystery is explained; the story is over.

The Story of Solution

Most "mystery stories" are really puzzle stories, the difference being that a mystery is explained by events, whereas a puzzle must be solved by the characters. In Lord Dunsany's "The Two Bottles of Relish," we know that a murder has occurred, but nobody can figure out how the body has been disposed of. The facts are these: The murderer is said to be a vegetarian. He bought two bottles of relish, six days apart. During the two weeks after the disappearance of his victim, he cut down ten larch trees and chopped them into two-foot lengths, but never burned them. He did not leave his home after the murder; the ground under and around his cottage has not been disturbed. Perhaps you have guessed the solution reached by the amateur detective in the story. But what about the trees—why did he cut them down? The last line of the story gives the answer:

"Solely," said Linley, "in order to get an appetite."

Readers of puzzle stories demand constant novelty—old solutions will not do. You probably should not attempt a puzzle story unless you have a taste for this kind of thing yourself and have read enough of it to have some idea of what other writers have done.

Stories about the approach of inevitable disaster form one exception to the rule that a plotted story must have an ending that is surprising in some way. Two examples are "Nightfall," by Isaac Asimov, and "Billenium," by J. G. Ballard. In both we can see exactly where the story is heading; there is no element of surprise, and yet these stories compel our attention in the same way that a natural disaster does. In "Nightfall," people on another planet go mad and burn their cities when the stars appear once every two thousand years. In "Billenium," two young men in an overcrowded world of the future discover a forgotten and boarded-up apartment. Unheard-of luxury! They invite their friends in to share it one by one and partition off the space until it is just as crowded as everywhere else.

Sometimes the inevitable ending is averted, as in Wells's *War of the Worlds,* by a rabbit-out-of-the-hat solution so transparent that the feeling of inevitability remains: if not this time, next time (the Martians will destroy us, or whatever).

In stories of this kind, a rather detached attitude toward the characters is probably a good thing: the reader ought to be able to sit back and observe the characters moving toward their doom, without becoming intimately involved. (Disasters are entertainment only when they happen to other people.)

Common Plotting Faults
and What to Do about Them

1. *Symptom:* Story line wanders, never seems to get anywhere.
   Diagnosis: Author has started writing the story without any clear idea of its direction.
   Treatment: Give your central character a stronger motivation and make things more difficult for her. Rewrite without looking at the old version.
2. *Symptom:* Story is confusing—too many characters, too much going on.
   Diagnosis: Author has not decided whose story this is, or has not found a way to focus the narrative on the central character.
   Treatment: Arbitrarily reduce the number of principal characters to three or four. Replot and rewrite.
3. *Symptom:* Plot structure looks complete, but the story seems curiously pointless.
   Diagnosis: Author has forgotten that we must care about the chief characters and it must matter what happens to them. Stories like this are often written by young people (usually male) who believe they have to plot mechanically in order to be published. Even in most popular fiction, in categories where plot is very important, the characters are more important. If you don't believe in your own characters and feel deeply about them, nobody else will either.
   Treatment: This is not a plot problem at all. Go back to characters and build from there.
4. *Symptom:* Ending is disappointing.
   Diagnosis: (1) Author has failed to misdirect the reader—the ending is disappointing because it is obvious; or (2) author has failed to plan ahead for the ending, hoping something would turn up, and in despair has tacked on a weak, irrelevant, or illogical ending.
   Treatment: It is useless to treat the ending by itself; any tacked-on ending will look tacked-on. Go back to the opening situation and replot.

Unplotted Stories

A plotted story has a skeletal structure that can be extracted and examined: the story makes sense if you just tell what happens in it. This is not true of unplotted stories. Consider, for example, Ernest Hemingway's "Big Two-Hearted River." It is easy to say what happens in this story. The narrator gets off a train in a deserted countryside and walks deep into the forest, where he makes camp and goes to sleep. In the morning he catches grasshoppers for bait, has breakfast, and fishes the river. He catches trout and cleans them. This account could be expanded by adding detail, but even if it included every least thing that happens, it would not tell you what the story means.

The strength of "Big Two-Hearted River" lies partly in its symbolism (the river is the narrator's life, and he is fishing the upper part of it, which represents the lost paradise of his boyhood), but there are powerful unplotted stories in which symbolism plays no part. Tolstoy's "The Death of Ivan Ilych" is simply the chronicle of a man's life; the same can be said of Willa Cather's "Neighbor Rosicky." In these stories we are profoundly moved, not by drama, but by the inner meaning of a human being's existence. These are stories of illumination rather than of revelation: they take the form, "This is what life is."

The story forms we have been discussing are not rigid little boxes, into which every work of fiction must be crammed; they are ideal categories. In practice, elements of these forms are mixed in all kinds of ways. The same story may be partly one of resolution, partly of revelation, partly of solution, partly of illumination (see, for example, *The Maltese Falcon,* by Dashiell Hammett). When you understand the simple forms, you can mix and combine them to make more sophisticated ones. There is no end to the stories that can be written, because the possible combinations of old forms will never be exhausted, and because good writers keep on inventing new forms.

Part 3

BEGINNING A STORY

When Is a Story Ready to Begin?

In L. Frank Baum's *Tik-Tok of Oz* there is a garden with a book tree in it. If you pick the books when they are ripe, they are full of exciting stories, but if you pick them green, the printing is blurred and the plots are muddled and dull. When I read student stories, I often say, "You picked this one too green."

For some people, a story is not ready to be written until it is completely worked out. Others begin writing with nothing but a situation and a set of characters; still others know the beginning and the end but have only a vague idea of what will happen in the middle.

Working the story out completely ahead of time is obviously the most efficient method, but it is one I can't use; if I knew that much about a story, I wouldn't want to write it. At the same time, I am too cautious to hurl myself into a story without a net. I want to know at least the general outline of the plot, including the ending, and a certain amount about the setting and all the characters, before I begin.

Something else that you will have to find out by trial and error is whether you can do all the planning for a story in your head, or whether it will help you to do some of it in the form of written notes. Sinclair Lewis wrote out elaborate biographical sketches of all his characters, even including their addresses and telephone numbers. Rex Stout, the creator of Nero Wolfe, said that the only thing he ever wrote down before beginning a novel was a list of the characters' names.

For years I never wrote anything down beforehand except a brief numbered list of scenes. Now I make a lot of notes; I write down everything that occurs to me, ask myself questions, list alternatives. Most of this is discarded, but it seems to me that it gives Fred something to work with, and it gives me little glimpses of what he is up to.

Like children, stories sometimes seem reluctant to be born, and then it becomes necessary to force them, but you should wait until you are sure the story is only reluctant, not unready. If you try to force it earlier, you will surround it with bits that don't belong to it organically and will stifle it. The story may be born, may be written, but it will never be what it should have been.

Any method that works for you is good. It is inefficient, certainly, to leap into a story without any idea where you will end up. V. S. Pritchett does that, and he says he has a drawer full of unfinished stories. But the stories he does finish are so marvelous that it would be absurd to tell him his method is wrong.

If, on the other hand, the method you are using is *not* working, if your stories are coming out muddled and dull because you haven't given them time enough to ripen, I would suggest that you try another method.

The Invisible Reader

Just as the invisible camera is part of every scene in a film, and every room in a play has an invisible fourth wall, so in fiction there is a convention that the reader is invisibly present in every scene. (So is the author, of course, and that means that the smallest possible number of characters in fiction is three.)

Every professional writer of fiction knows this in his bones, even if he has never once thought about it. Many beginning writers don't know it. Their stories are impenetrable, because they have left no room for the reader to enter them. An editor looks at the first page of a story written in this way, finds she "can't get into it," doesn't know why, but doesn't need to know why—she slides a rejection slip under the paper clip, stuffs the manuscript into the return envelope, and that's that.

Look at it this way: you're the author, and your role is that of host; the reader is your guest. As a matter of ordinary courtesy, you open the door and welcome him in, and then you show him around, introduce the other people present, explain things that may be confusing to him. You stay with him, making sure always that he has a good view of what's going on and that he has enough information to understand it.

If there is no reader—if you, the author, are alone with your characters—then of course none of this is necessary. *You* know who the characters are and what they're doing, and there's no need to explain. But if you assume there's no reader, you're right, because nobody will ever read your story all the way through except your nearest and dearest relatives. (Even they may skip.)

Imagine, as you write, that a reader is at your elbow, constantly commenting on what she sees and asking questions.

He opened the door and found himself in a room.

(How big a room?)

He opened the door and found himself in a long, narrow room. (Anybody in it?)

He opened the door and found himself in a long, narrow room full of people.

(How were they dressed?)

He opened the door and found himself in a long, narrow room full of people in evening dress.

(What were they doing?)

He opened the door and found himself in a long, narrow room full of people in evening dress with drinks in their hands. A man came up to him.

(What did he look like?)

A bald man with a broken nose came up to him, frowning.

Here are some other questions to ask yourself as you think about a story. You will have to know the answers to these questions at some point, and you can save yourself a lot of grief if you know them before you start to write.

Five Questions

Who is the story about?

Why are they doing what they're doing?

What is the story about?

Where does the story take place?

When does the story take place?

You should answer at least four of these questions as early as possible in the story—preferably within the first two hundred words. ("Why" can often come a little later.) Otherwise you will probably fail to give the reader a coherent image to focus his attention on, and that's fatal.

The Characters: Who Is the Story About?

And why should we be interested in these people? You must tell us enough, immediately, to accomplish two things:

To make it clear that you, the author, know your characters intimately.

To make us feel something about them—curiosity, sympathy, antipathy—anything but indifference.

Otherwise, why should we bother to read on?

In the beginning you will probably be tempted to copy your characters either from characters in other people's fiction or from people you know. Since the most complex characters in fiction are impossible to imitate, you will find yourself copying the simplest characters and turning them into stereotypes or caricatures.

Copying characters from real people carries two hazards with it. It often happens that you know the person you are describing so well that you fail to tell the reader enough about her—*you* see her and hear her talking when you read what you have written, and you assume wrongly that the reader will too. There is an opposite danger, that you will put in too much of what you know about the person—he is a dentist, he lives on Elm Street, he has three children and an Airedale, etc., when all you really want of him is his ruddy cheeks, his optimism, and his habit of giving unasked-for advice. The trick is to use bits and pieces of real people, combined in new ways, in order to create characters who are not copies of anyone.

Here are some other devices you can use to train yourself to create characters.

1. Write a brief biographical sketch of each one—date and place of birth, parents, education, work history, and so on. This sketch,

like any other creative writing, should be done in collaboration with Fred. If you simply invent details at random, you will probably wind up feeling that you really don't know this character and don't want to write about her.

2. Write a description of the character as seen by another character in the story. If there are a number of characters in the story, you may find it useful and illuminating to write at least *two* descriptions of each character, as seen by different people. This exercise will sharpen your own understanding of your characters, by forcing you to see each one from at least two directions. It will also help you form the habit of thinking of every character as a real, living person, not a piece of stage furniture.

3. Write a scene in which the character comes home and does whatever he routinely does at that time of day. What does he do first—light a cigarette? Water the plants? Feed the parrot? Or what?

4. Write an incident in the character's life which you will not use in the story, but which reveals something about her.

5. Invent a second character who is like the first in a general way—another restless teenager, or whatever—and write a scene between the two (again, something you will not use in the story). The scene must show the differences between the two characters in their attitudes, the way they talk, etc. If they sound so much alike that you can't tell the difference except for their names, write it over—and over, until you *can* tell the difference. If you are having trouble with this, it is a clue that your first character is a stereotype. (Maybe your second character will come to life before the first one does; if so, give him the job.)

Each time you write a scene from the viewpoint of one of your characters, imagine yourself inside that person's head. Exactly what is that person seeing right now—what is she hearing? What other sensations is she aware of? What is she thinking? Remembering? What impulses does she suppress? What does she notice while another person is speaking? What is her mood? Is she elated, depressed, or what?

Now put yourself into the head of the next most important character in the scene: what is *his* motive for behaving as he does? What is he seeing, feeling, etc.? Go back to your central character, and play the scene all over again from her point of view. What she sees, hears, and feels may be drastically altered, because you now know more about the second character.

Try to remember that your subsidiary characters are not unimportant to themselves. Each one is the center of his own drama; each one should be so real to you that if you chose, you could write a story about him.

Your best source of information about what makes people behave the way they do, you may be glad to hear, is yourself. By the time you are sixteen (Jean Piaget, the developmental psychologist, says by the time you are *six*) you have experienced every human emotion. Is your character behaving selfishly? Look into yourself: you'll find selfishness. Or courage, or malice, or devotion, or envy—it's all there, and you can use it to create believable characters. (This is great therapy, by the way.)

If you have known a person for years, and especially if you live with that person, you don't notice the same details about her that you would notice if you were meeting her for the first time. For this reason the most effective viewpoint character is often a visitor, someone to whom the characters and the setting are fresh. But there are ways to tell the reader what he needs to know even when you are using the viewpoint of a character long familiar with other characters. At moments of strong affection, for instance, we notice all over again how beautiful a person is, and at moments of irritation we see her faults as if for the first time.

Whenever a person is doing something unusual, or when there is something unusual about his appearance, we look him over carefully. These moments give us an opportunity to describe a character vividly without making the reader wonder why our viewpoint character, who sees this person every day, is noticing all that.

Resist the impulse to stereotype your characters according to their occupations or their media images. The reader can do that himself; why should he pay you to do it? Let's say your character is a police sergeant with almost twenty years' experience. He need not be a wrestling fan, a beer drinker, or a Republican. He may be a Marxist and a Transcendental Meditation student who breeds dahlias and has a child bride. Give your characters credit for being as complex and interesting as you are, and give them a little slack. Listen to what Fred has to say about them; find out what *they* want to do. Often they will improve your plot for you.

If you're not sure about your central character's motivation, it may be helpful to write a scene, entirely in dialogue, between your character and an interrogator who asks questions like, "Why did you do that?" If the character doesn't answer truthfully, the interrogator keeps pressing him until he does.

Naming Your Characters

Names of characters in fiction should be realistic—that is, they should be the sort of names that real people have, within the limits of credibility and taste; they should be reasonably easy to distinguish from one another (meaning, for instance, that no two should sound alike or begin with the same letter), and they should be appropriate to the characters. Choose one way of referring to each character and stick to it as much as possible. If a man's name is Tim Benko, for instance, don't call him Benko for two pages and then switch to Tim.

If you are inventing names as you go along, and coming up with a lot of Robinsons, Coopers, and Smiths, you are impoverishing your work and perpetuating a WASP image of the world. If the real people you know have names that reflect all kinds of national origins, why should your characters all have Anglo-Saxon names?

Telephone books are poor sources of names when you're in a hurry, because it takes too long to get through one letter of the alphabet. You might try keeping a list of names that catch your eye when you use the phone book; that list, being mixed alphabetically, will be more useful. Always write down the full name, "Lenore E. Birnbaum," for instance, not just "Lenore" or "Birnbaum," to make sure you won't unconsciously restore the missing half when you use the name. (People whose names are used in fiction sometimes sue.)

When you want an authentic-sounding name for a citizen of a foreign country, one good source is the bibliographic notes after the article on that country in the encyclopedia. These will usually include references to books written by obscure scholars, whereas the article itself will be full of famous names.

It is dangerous to use U.S. telephone books for this purpose, because people in this country alter their names in all kinds of ways; a person whose grandfather was German may have a name that would never be found in Germany.

Three Exercises in Character

1. Write a story about some painful episode in your own life, but transfer it to an invented person distinctly different from yourself. Change the character's sex, age, occupation, or all three. Adapt the episode to your character's nature and circumstances. In the process, you may find that you have to change it so much that no one but yourself would know they are the same. You will also rid yourself of the confusing mass of nonessential detail that belongs to the real episode, and you will retreat so far from the episode that you can write freely about it.

2. If you are a woman, write a complete story from a man's viewpoint. If you are a man, write a complete story from a woman's viewpoint. (If you are one of those rare writers who habitually uses the viewpoint of the opposite sex, reverse this.)

3. Think of someone in your past for whom you felt only anger and hatred. Write a story from the viewpoint of that person, *treated with sympathy.*

These exercises are designed to break you out of any easy rut you may have got yourself into—writing only about people of one sex, or only about pleasant things, or only about people who resemble you. Unless you force yourself to do harder things, how will you grow?

Motivation: Why Are These People Doing What They're Doing?

If the answer is, "Because the story wouldn't work if they didn't," you are in deep trouble. Forget about your reason—what's *their* reason?

Motives must be proportional in seriousness and intensity to the risks that people take and the trouble they cause for themselves and others. If your characters' motives are trivial, their actions will be either trivial or incredible.

If the story is one of conflict, give your characters something *important* to win or lose—life, money, love, freedom, self-respect; or, if not one of these, something that *to your character* is equally important. If he wants a million dollars, you don't need to explain that, but if he is mortgaging everything he owns and risking his marriage and his career in order to buy a set of Queen Victoria's underwear, you must draw your character so vividly that we can believe in his actions. (Unless you can understand this kind of obsession yourself, you probably can't.)

In a puzzle story, simple curiosity is motive enough. Don't underrate curiosity—it is one of the strongest human drives. We read stories at least partly to satisfy our curiosity about how other people live, about foreign lands and hazardous occupations—about everything that is outside our own experience. We read stories to satisfy our curiosity about life in the future and on other planets, even though we know the authors are making it all up. Curiosity keeps us turning pages: How did the murderer get into the locked room? Will Rhett leave Scarlett? Who is that masked man?

In a story of mystery, the central character usually doesn't know what is happening; she does what she does because she is helpless to do anything else. Since her actions are dictated by events, her motivation is no problem, but you must be all the more careful to motivate the people who *do* know what's happening. If they have contrived a vast deception or conspiracy in which the heroine finds herself enmeshed, what is *their* motive? They must have something important to gain, or they wouldn't go to all that trouble. If it turns out in the end that the author has failed to give the villains any real motive, the story collapses and the reader feels cheated.

Think of motivation in cost-benefit terms. No matter how difficult or bizarre your character's desire may be, you can make it plausible for him to seek it if you are able to show that *to him* it is worth what it costs.

"You Must Help Us!"

When a minor character (A) comes to the central character (B) and says, "You must help us!" it is almost always a sign that you have the wrong central character. In the first place, it's A who has the problem and A who ought to resolve it; what is B doing in this story to begin with? In the second place, *why* must B help A? What's in it for B? If the answer is "Nothing," you have an unmotivated central character. You can't count on much sympathy from the reader if B helps A and in the process gets into trouble, because he knows that B doesn't have to be there—she can get out any time and mind her own business. (People do help other people, even when it is inconvenient or dangerous, but there is always a reason.)

These remarks do not apply to comic books or television serials.

The Subject: What Is the Story About?

What people want when they ask this question is not the essential or philosophical subject of the story ("love and death," for instance), but something more immediate and practical: the story is about a man undergoing a midlife crisis, for instance ("The Country Husband," by John Cheever), or it's about an attractive, accommodating woman ("Big Blonde," by Dorothy Parker), or a brutal murder ("Markheim," by Robert Louis Stevenson), or a peculiar marriage ("The Boarding House," by James Joyce).

When you begin reading Maugham's story "Rain" for the first time, you don't know that it's about a struggle between a missionary and a prostitute, but you do know it's about the passengers on a ship in the South Seas, and that's enough. (Notice too that although the real subject of the story does not appear in the opening, it is evoked in various subtle ways—"the harsh note of the mechanical piano," for instance, a sound that will take on more meaning later.)

If the opening of your story doesn't give the reader *any* answer to the question, "What is it about?" the chances are she will never turn the page.

The Setting: Where Does the Story Take Place?

Setting is the visible part of the background of a story. Think of it as a stage setting, if you like: the curtain goes up, there is the protagonist's living room—her worn couch with a Guatemalan throw rug over it, her travel posters on the wall, the stereo and records in one corner, the Sunday *Times* on the floor, and through her windows you can see the fire escape and the smoky skyline of lower Manhattan. No one has walked on stage so far, and yet you already know something about the person who lives here.

In a wider sense, setting means locale—the part of the world where the story takes place. Some people tell you quite sincerely that in this sense, setting must govern story, meaning that the story must grow out of the setting and that it must be one that could not take place anywhere else.

There is a story of John O'Hara's, "I Spend My Days in Longing," which takes place entirely in a hotel room that might be in Cleveland or Chicago or Cincinnati, and in fact that's the point: one of the two characters can't remember what city they're in now. Tolstoy's "The Death of Ivan Ilych" takes place in St. Petersburg, but with minor changes it could have been set in nineteenth-century Paris or London, and the story would have been just the same. What does seem to be true is that the setting or locale ought to have some visible relation to the story, to be appropriate to it. Don't use an exotic setting (the South Seas, or a colony on the Moon) for a story that could just as well take place in San Diego. If the people and their problems are familiar, the setting should be familiar too.

An Exercise in Setting As Character

Take a character from one of your own stories, or invent a new one, and describe the living room of her house or apartment as if it were an empty stage setting, in such a way that we can learn a good deal about the character just by looking at the place where she lives. Remember that you are not allowed to make any direct statement about the character ("Linda loved luxury," for instance). Write only what you see.

Background Minus Setting

Background in fiction includes everything that is not front and center—everything that is not foreground. It includes landscape, architecture, and climate, and it also includes such things as the culture in which the story takes place, the past lives of the characters, the history of the nation or community in which they live, its sociology, technology, philosophy, arts, manners, and so on.

In contemporary fiction nearly all of this is taken for granted, assumed by both writer and reader; the reader will fill in a good deal of the background for you if you merely say "Manhattan," or "Miami Beach," or whatever. But also, if you make any mistakes, she will catch you at it. You will need specific, convincing details to give the reader confidence that you really know the place you're writing about and are not relying on general impressions from TV or movies.

See my earlier remarks about describing people who are well known to your viewpoint character; the same principle applies here. A longtime resident of Manhattan does not ordinarily notice the landmarks that would attract a visitor—he takes them for granted. He doesn't give much thought to the World Trade Towers, or the Statue of Liberty—he is more interested in the people behind the counter in the coffee shop where he eats breakfast every morning. What does that coffee shop look like—how is it different from a coffee shop in Albuquerque, or one in Seattle? Is the waitress patient and slow-moving, or quick and irritable? What newspapers are the customers reading? What is the quality of the light?

If the background is invented, as in a fantasy or science-fiction story, then you have a good deal more work to do, but the only things you have to worry about are scientific (or magical) possibility and self-consistency. You have not been to Aldebaran IV or Elfland, but neither has your reader, and if you are reasonably plausible she can't call you a liar.

Don't copy anyone else's background, no matter how sincerely you admire it. The author you admire has abstracted the details you see from hundreds of others; the background is vivid precisely because the author knows much more than he has set down. If you now take this as your model, you will have to abstract again, and the result will be a grainy imitation, like a Xerox of a photograph. (Every time you copy, some information is lost.)

The Expository Lump and How to Avoid It

You can't describe any scene fully; there isn't room enough. You must learn the art of what Robin Wilson calls "furnishing the world on a budget."

Give a strong general impression if you can ("the vaultlike room was full of echoes"), and then a few salient details (*"¡Venceremos!* was spray-painted on the wall; under it someone had written, *Like hell"*). If they are well chosen, the reader will fill in the rest. The same goes for characters. Don't try to describe them so minutely that an artist could paint their portraits; detailed description actually irritates many readers because it interferes with their own image-making. A word or two about each character when she first appears or shortly thereafter will do: old or young? tall or short, fat or thin? blond or brunet? Don't save any of these revelations for page 20; if you suddenly tell us the heroine is blond, while we have been visualizing her as brunet, you have given us an unpleasant jolt.

For the same reason, beware of being specific too late about such things as right and left, east and west. If the hero has been climbing a mountain ledge for the last three pages, and then you tell us he looks down to his right, we may have to turn him around. Interfere as little as possible with the reader's imaginative creation of the story.

Most of the time you will not want or need to describe any setting in great detail, but it is a mistake to think that for that reason you don't need to know it. You should know where the kitchen cabinets are and what's in them; you should know how the house is laid out. All this will give you confidence that will be felt by the reader, even if little of it appears directly in the story. It will also forestall embarrassing errors, as when a character goes directly from the kitchen to the dining room on page 10, but has to go through the hall to reach it on page 32.

Write, if you like, detailed descriptions of settings and characters, biographical sketches, and so on, but don't put them verbatim into the story. An undigested mass of information of this kind is called an *expository lump,* and it is an obstacle that many readers are unwilling to climb over. If you know the background thoroughly, it will expose itself piecemeal in the course of the action. Suppose you are writing a story about the New York subway. You may begin with a page and a half about the construction, history, and mode of operation of the New York subway system; that will be an expository lump. Or you may take your viewpoint character down through the turnstile onto the platform, describing what she sees as you go. By the time she comes up again a mile away, your reader will know all he needs to know about the subway.

A good writer can get away with an expository lump if it is there for a reason—for instance, if the plot turns on some scientific discovery that must be made comprehensible to the reader. More often, especially in student writing, the author has used the lump out of laziness or lack of skill. Lecture the reader *only* if there's no better way.

What's Outside the Frame

In order to paint a convincing picture of a landscape or a city street, you must know *what's outside the frame.* Therefore, don't stop when you have invented the parts of the background that will show in the story. If the action takes place in a room, what's outside that room? What does the building next door look like? What kind of street is this; what kind of neighborhood? If you know all this, it will be reflected in the way your characters behave: for instance, they won't talk about taking a taxi home if this is a slum neighborhood where cab drivers refuse to go.

Clear a Space

Every inch of the real world is full of real people and real things; there is no room in it for fictional people and things. What you must do in order to write "realistic" fiction is to clear a space for it—make room in the heart of Chicago or in Kalamazoo or wherever you like for your imagined characters to meet and react to each other. Be ruthless: if all the clerks and secretaries and vice-presidents on two floors of a real skyscraper have to go, out with them. If you want the mayor's office, take it. You may want to use a real office or bank, exactly as it is, and clear out all the people in it to make room for your characters: or you may want to scrape a whole county off the map and replace it with one of your own, as William Faulkner did in his stories of "Yoknapatawpha County." Cover your tracks carefully, surround your cleared space with real places and things, and then do exactly as you please.

The Period: When Does the Story Take Place?

For most writers the automatic answer is "Now," but in science fiction and period fiction there are other answers, and they bring problems of their own. (In period fiction they are mainly problems of research; in fantasy and science fiction they are mainly problems of invention.) Your story is set in New York in the late 1940s, and two of your characters are having a drink in a bar on Third Avenue. Is the El still there or not? Look it up. Or your story is set in San Francisco thirty years in the future. How has the city changed? What urban projects were being talked about in your own time? Did they succeed or fail? What has happened to the country, to the world? Is this a period of boom or bust? What significant advances in technology have been made, and how have they affected living patterns, transportation, politics?

Think of the contrast between the San Francisco of today and the San Francisco of thirty years ago. Project that into the future—show us a city changed at least that much (more, really, because the *rate* of change has been increasing).

- How do your characters get from one place to another?
- What kind of work do they do?
- What do they do for entertainment?
- How do they dress?

If your San Francisco of the future is just like the present city, in these and all other ways, the reader will know you haven't done your homework. You don't eat, wear, or read exactly the same things your parents did. If you go back to a town you knew well only twenty years ago, the chances are that you won't even recognize it. When you take us into the future, or to another planet, you must give us a sense of change, of difference.

Four Choices

Consciously or otherwise, you will make four choices about the beginning of every story. You will choose the place to begin, the viewpoint, the person (first, second, or third), and the tense.

Where to Begin

The opening is especially important and difficult because it has to stand on its own; every other part of the story has the preceding parts to lean on. The opening must establish character, setting, situation, the mood and tone of the story; it must provoke interest, arouse curiosity, suggest conflict, start the movement of the plot—all this in about two hundred words.

What is the right place to begin? Usually it is a moment not too long before the first important event of the narrative, but not too close to it either. If you begin with your principal character's childhood, and tell us all about her toys, her favorite teachers, her measles, mumps, and whooping cough, the reader may lose patience before you ever get near the love story or spy story or whatever it was that you set out to write. On the other hand, if you plunge instantly into the action, you risk losing the reader in another way. It is hard to take much interest in absolute strangers, no matter how enthusiastically they may be bashing each other.

Another reason for beginning before the first important event of the narrative, particularly if that event involves some unusual behavior on the part of the central character, is to *establish a baseline* by showing how your character behaves under normal circumstances. Without this, it may be hard to interpret his behavior under stress.

There is a school of thought that says you must always grab your reader's attention immediately, by the use of a "narrative hook"—an opening sentence so arresting that your reader is compelled to go on with the story:

> "Look!" I shouted. "They're coming through the ceiling!"

Look is a word that automatically draws our attention; *you* is another. (Notice how often I use it in these pages.)

After the hook, for good measure, you may toss in a few more arresting statements just to make sure the reader doesn't get away:

> She had clothes on, but they covered her about as well as
> a postage stamp covers an envelope.

I had better admit that I dislike these methods; when I was young it was different, but nowadays if I look at the beginning of a story and find that the author is trying to grab me by the lapels, I go away and leave her to clutch somebody else. My feeling now is that if the author has something interesting to say, she can capture my attention by saying it. I like beginnings that introduce me into the story gently and gradually, and I try to write that way myself.

Even if you use an attention-getting first sentence, it should contain some information. (In the first example above, we know that *something* is coming through the ceiling. We expect that the following sentences will tell us more. If they do, and if the situation continues to be interesting, we'll keep reading.)

However you begin, it is important to let the reader know what *kind* of story this is going to be. The first paragraph is like the first spoonful of a new kind of ice cream. People often turn the pages of a magazine or a collection of stories, tasting first paragraphs until they find one they like. If the story is going to be one of action and suspense, the first paragraph should suggest that; if it is going to be an intriguing study of character, that should be indicated too.

At any rate, every story-opening problem will have its own best solution, which you must find by trial and error (throw away beginnings until you get the one that feels right). The opening ought to be roughly proportional to the length of the story. In a story of five thousand words or less, the first important event probably ought to take place not later than page 2 or 3; in a story twice that long it may be delayed somewhat. But drama and tension should in any event be suggested, hinted at, within the first two hundred words.

Mystery is the essence of storytelling, but pointless mystification is just a pain in the neck. (One of your characters, who tells the story in the first person, has an unheard-of and unpronounceable name. Partly because of this, we don't find out he is a male until page 5. Or your central character is a Skid Row bum who is referred to throughout as the Dalai Lama. Is he the Dalai Lama disguised as a bum, or a bum who thinks he is the Dalai Lama? Or what? You never explain, and we never find out.)

Scrutinize your first page for terms and references that are not explained and are not self-explanatory. Even one of these is probably too many; if there are five or six, you are in trouble. Don't overwhelm the reader with strange characters and settings. Treat him as a courteous host would, introducing him to one or two people at a time.

Don't begin a story with a quotation mark unless you can quickly establish who is speaking and to whom. Better yet, precede the first line of dialogue with one or two descriptive or narrative sentences.

An Exercise in Openings

Write two story beginnings, each no more than five or six lines long. Try to make each one as attractive as possible to the prospective reader. Make sure that what you write is strongly focused and fluent. In the first, use as many attention-getting devices as you like, in order to capture the reader by intriguing her curiosity. In the second, try to accomplish the same thing by developing the setting, character, and situation, without any conspicuous tricks or flashiness.

Don't worry at this stage whether you can finish the stories or not.

Viewpoint

Maybe viewpoint is so difficult for many beginning writers because it is a relatively recent invention and hasn't had time to get under our skins. For thousands of years the only point of view was that of the person who was telling the story. It never occurred to anybody to pretend that he could know what another person was thinking. The narrator did not hesitate to report what the gods were doing, and he often explained the reasons for the characters' actions, freely blaming or praising them, but the story itself was "what happened"—what the characters said and did.

When printed books became common and inexpensive, the tellers of tales discovered that they had lost certain advantages and gained others. The narrator was no longer physically present when his story was told, and that was bad because he no longer had the power of his voice or the rhythms of his harp; but it was good because he could assume any disguise he liked, place himself in the foreground of the story or retire, even become invisible.

For a long time, nevertheless, written stories resembled oral tales. Even when writers ventured to reveal, briefly, what their characters were thinking, the story was still a thing told by the narrator and it had no other point of view. Selma Lagerlöf's "A Christmas Guest" is like this. The story is about a retired violinist who has driven off an unwelcome guest on Christmas Eve and is feeling remorseful. Then the guest comes back.

> Liljekrona went on with the wild playing up in his room; he did not know that Ruster had come. The latter sat meanwhile in the dining room with the wife and the children. The servants, who used also to be there on Christmas Eve, moved out into the kitchen away from their mistress's trouble.

Here, in a single paragraph, we have the violinist in his room, the guest, the wife, and the children in the dining room, and the servants in the kitchen; and if the author had felt like bringing in the handyman in the cellar or the cat in the attic, she could have done that too.

This method is marvelously economical, but it is diffuse; the only thing that holds it together is the narrative itself, and that means usually that the story has to be a fairly simple one.

In order to tell more complex stories, writers began to use viewpoints that were narrower and sharper: the **omniscient** viewpoint, in which the author can enter any character's mind; **limited omni-**

scient, in which he can enter the mind of only one; the **detached** viewpoint, in which he refrains from entering any character's mind; and finally the **single-character** viewpoint, in which the story is told entirely through the perceptions of one character.

I'm going to try to disentangle this subject for you by discussing each different kind of viewpoint separately, as if every story were written entirely in one or the other, although in practice it is not always like that.

The Omniscient Viewpoint

The omniscient author still has the tale-teller's power to condense or summarize events and to move freely among the characters. She can go into the central character's mind, to show what he is thinking and feeling; then she can drift out and look at him quite objectively and even with amusement. She can look at other characters objectively, too, or she can dip into their minds and show them as they really are—not necessarily as the central character sees them.

It was nearly bed-time and when they awoke next morning land would be in sight. Dr. Macphail lit his pipe and, leaning over the rail, searched the heavens for the Southern Cross. After two years at the front and a wound that had taken longer to heal than it should, he was glad to settle down quietly at Apia for twelve months at least, and he felt already better for the journey. Since some of the passengers were leaving the ship next day at Pago-Pago they had had a little dance that evening and in his ears hammered still the harsh notes of the mechanical piano. But the deck was quiet at last. A little way off he saw his wife in a long chair talking with the Davidsons, and he strolled over to her. When he sat down under the light and took off his hat you saw that he had very red hair, with a bald patch on the crown, and the red, freckled skin which accompanies red hair; he was a man of forty, thin, with a pinched face, precise and rather pedantic; and he spoke with a Scots accent in a very low, quiet voice.

"Rain," by W. Somerset Maugham

This story begins with a general statement that might be in almost any viewpoint, from Dr. Macphail's to that of the omniscient author. In the third sentence the viewpoint dips into the mind of Dr. Macphail ("he felt already better for the journey"), and then, when Macphail approaches his wife, it draws back a little in order to inspect him from the outside ("very red hair, with a bald patch on the crown . . ."), and so on.

As the story develops, the viewpoint often returns to the mind of Dr. Macphail, but never stays there long, and it dips at one time or another into the mind of every other important character, with the single exception of the missionary, Mr. Davidson. This circling movement focuses our attention on the hidden struggle between the missionary and Miss Thompson, where it belongs, whereas if only the viewpoint of Dr. Macphail had been used, he would have come awkwardly into the foreground.

The drifting omniscient viewpoint can perform a stately dance that is pleasing in itself, and it tends to give us a curious semi-detached involvement, almost like a God's-eye view. We are in and out of people's heads so often that we seldom feel trapped in any one person, and therefore the omniscient viewpoint does not usually raise our anxiety as much as the single- or multiple-character viewpoints can. (The omniscient viewpoint would not be the obvious choice for a suspense story, in which we want the reader to feel as much anxiety as possible.) The omniscient viewpoint is serene, slow-moving, contemplative. For these and other reasons, genre fiction seldom uses it.

Limited Omniscient

This phrase, which sounds like (and is) a contradiction in terms, describes the viewpoint that can do anything the omniscient viewpoint can, except that it can enter the mind of only one character. (In the Maugham story, if the author had never entered the mind of any character other than Dr. Macphail, that would have been limited omniscient.)

This viewpoint is useful when you don't want to look into the mind of more than one character, but you do want to describe your central character both from the inside and the outside. Once you have done this in the opening paragraph or two, you may have got all you wanted from the limited omniscient viewpoint, and in that case you can slide unobtrusively into a single-character viewpoint and stay there.

The Detached Viewpoint

Detached-viewpoint stories are those in which we never get into the head of any character; we are simply floating, invisible observers.

In John O'Hara's "A Purchase of Some Golf Clubs," a young man comes into a bar and talks to the bartender, then to a young woman who is trying to sell a set of golf clubs. The opening is written in such a way that we might expect the viewpoint to become that of the young man, but that never happens. O'Hara simply records what all three characters say and do.

The difference between this and the "narrator viewpoint" I talked about earlier is that the narrator has disappeared; rather than feeling that the story is being told to you by somebody, you have the impression that you are seeing and hearing the events as they take place, as if you were present but invisible in the room.

This viewpoint is often called "camera eye," but the term is misleading. "Camera eye," we are told, is a viewpoint in which the reader is allowed to see only what a camera would see and hear what a microphone would hear, as in the work of Dashiell Hammett.

> Miss Wonderly watched the gray flakes twitch and crawl.
> Her eyes were uneasy. She sat on the very edge of the chair.
> Her feet were flat on the floor, as if she were about to rise.
>
> *The Maltese Falcon*

"Her eyes were uneasy." ". . . as if she were about to rise." These are comments, interpretations. A camera can't comment or interpret. Even the word *she* or the word *watched* has no meaning to a camera. What Hammett does, and does superbly, is to make the reader feel that she is an invisible observer there in the room with Miss Wonderly and Sam Spade.

The detached viewpoint is the closest thing in fiction to the performance of a stage play: we see and hear everything that happens, but we never get inside the head of any character. Because of these severe limitations, the detached viewpoint has a purity that appeals to me strongly. John O'Hara used this viewpoint better than anyone else I know; if you want to study it, read any of his story collections.

Please notice as we go along how the viewpoints are becoming narrower and sharper. Your choice of viewpoints will be determined by how much you want the reader to see, and in what detail—you will choose a viewpoint as a photographer might choose a lens for the particular job he has to do. The omniscient viewpoints are like wide-angle lenses; the detached viewpoint is like a telephoto lens—it can observe sharply, but from a distance; and the single- and multiple-person viewpoints are like portrait lenses.

The Single-Character Viewpoint

This viewpoint imposes a drastic limitation on the writer—she can report *only* what the viewpoint character thinks, feels, perceives, etc.—but it has compensating advantages. It is much less diffuse than the omniscient or limited-omniscient viewpoint usually is. By concentrating on one character, it can draw the reader into a strong identification with that character.

Sometimes the viewpoint character is an invented narrator who tells what amounts to a story within a story. Sometimes she speaks in the first person directly to the reader; sometimes she writes the story as a memoir. These devices often complicate the story without improving it much, but they may be useful when the author wants to keep a distance between the central character and the reader (usually because the central character is a mystery, as in *The Great Gatsby,* by F. Scott Fitzgerald).

Identification with the central character is strongly desired by readers of commercial fiction. A woman reading a romance novel wants to imagine herself as the heroine and live through the latter's adventures vicariously. A man reading a Western story wants to imagine himself tall in the saddle. This kind of reader identification with the protagonist is hard to achieve in any but a single-character viewpoint. Commercial short fiction, therefore, almost always uses this viewpoint, whereas in "serious" fiction the omniscient viewpoints are more frequent.

In third person, the single-character viewpoint can be either subjective or objective. (This is true of first and second person, too, but strictly objective writing in the first two persons is rare.) In the subjective mode, you can tell us what the viewpoint character thinks, feels, remembers, etc., in addition to what he sees and hears, but you can't tell us what he looks like, and you can't tell us anything he doesn't know. In the objective mode, you can tell us what the character looks like and describe everything he can see and hear, but you can't tell us anything *directly* about his feelings, internal sensations, or thoughts.

To illustrate, here is a brief passage written in third person subjective:

> James Maxwell opened the cool iron gate, stepped in and closed it behind him. On either side of the walk, tall masses of white blooms hung heavy and sweet. The stone house was silent, the blinds closed like eyelids. There was a sour taste in his mouth; his belly rumbled. Lousy slum they gave you in that hotel coffee shop; serve them right if he went to hospital and sued them. He listened, heard the *wheep, wheep* of a lawn sprinkler somewhere off to his right. He wondered uneasily what Julia was doing now—was she in her morning room, bent over her accounts? He could still hear the last words she had spoken to him: "Never mind about hard feelings, Jim. Just don't come back."
>
> His throat was dry. He started up the walk, hearing his own footsteps click unpleasantly on the flagstones.

Now here is the same passage written in third person objective. Notice the difference in the information content of the two passages, even though the scene and action are the same as before.

> James Morton Maxwell opened a wrought-iron gate, stepped inside, and closed it behind him. He was a man in his

forties, red-faced and stout, with a ragged blond mustache. His yellow hair, badly trimmed, stood out in moist spikes under the brim of his Panama hat. The lapels of his seersucker jacket were wrinkled. From where he stood, a flagstone path led between tall mock orange bushes, heavy with blooms, to the entrance of a gray stone house. The blinds were shut.

Maxwell stood in a listening attitude. There was no sound except for the *wheep, wheep* of a lawn sprinkler somewhere off to the right. In Maxwell's protuberant eyes as he looked up at the house there was something indecisive, perhaps a touch of fear. He moistened his lips, started heavily up the walk.

Some of the differences between these two passages are obvious. In the subjective passage we are able to characterize Maxwell by getting into his head (and his stomach), but we can't describe him physically. Notice also that in the objective passage we are able to name the shrubs (mock orange), but not in the subjective passage, because Maxwell is not the sort of man who would know one shrub from another.

Which of these two modes is best for our purpose? That depends on what we want in the story. If we use a subjective viewpoint for Maxwell, he will come more into the foreground than Julia does. Is that what we want or not? Can we get more mileage out of Maxwell's facial expressions or his thoughts? What are we going to find inside Julia's house, and will it be easier to describe it from inside or outside Maxwell's mind? When Maxwell does whatever he is going to do, will we have to tell what he's thinking in order to make his motives clear? Our decision will probably be made by taste and instinct, but if the story works, it will be possible to look back and see the reasons.

The Multiple-Character Viewpoint

This is nothing but a series of single-character episodes strung together, each with a different viewpoint character. It is useful when the story cannot be told from a single viewpoint because no one character can be in all the places where the story has to go. It differs from the omniscient viewpoint in that each single-character episode is of some length—the viewpoint doesn't jump back and forth within a single paragraph as the omniscient viewpoint can.

The multiple-character viewpoint is a natural way of writing for me; I use it in preference to the omniscient or limited-omniscient viewpoint because it seems to me that it gives me all the sharp, portraitlike quality of the single-person viewpoint, and nearly as much panoramic wideness as the omniscient. When a story can be told from a single viewpoint, I tell it that way; otherwise I use multiple. This is at least partly a matter of temperament. I like to get as close to the central character as the story will let me—you may prefer to stay back and drift around.

Which Viewpoint Is Best?

Think of the young woman in the cabin again. She is the obvious viewpoint character, but you might get still more tension (and surprise the reader) by using the viewpoint of whoever is out there watching her through the windows.

Which *person* will you use, once you have chosen a viewpoint character? Third is the most obvious ("The prowler crept closer to the cabin, his eyes glittering in the moonlight"), but first person might heighten the mystery, because it tells so little about the viewpoint character ("I watched her tonight for an hour while she sat reading a book," etc.); or you might surprise us even more by using second person. ("After dinner you washed your dishes and left them to drain. You opened a book and put it down, then went to the window; but you saw nothing.") Here the existence of the prowler outside the cabin is implied but never stated—that might make him even more unnerving.

The *obvious* solution to any writing problem is always suspect: what is obvious to you is likely to be obvious to the reader too.

Viewpoint Switches

One of the most characteristic beginner's errors is the viewpoint switch—a sudden and unnecessary change from one viewpoint to another, of which, usually, the writer is not even aware.

David was looking over the menu, trying to decide what to order. He didn't feel much like anything heavy. "I'll just have a club sandwich," he said.

"And something to drink?" the waitress asked. She looked at him admiringly. Gee, he sure is handsome, she thought.

This excerpt is taken from page 3 of the story. Up until this moment we have been in David's viewpoint; suddenly and for no particular reason we find ourselves in the mind of the waitress. Later on, as David talks to his lunch companion, Mark, we will bounce like a shuttlecock between David's viewpoint and Mark's, again for no particular reason.

But, you will say, if all these changes would have been permissible if the story had been in the omniscient viewpoint, what's the difference?

1. A story written in the omniscient viewpoint always claims its territory in the first few pages by letting us see at least one character both from the inside and outside. (See, for instance, the opening of Maugham's "Rain.") The beginner's story quoted above does not do this; it begins as if it were a single-character viewpoint story, David's, and then jars us by shifting into the minds of other characters.

2. In a well-written omniscient story, there is a reason for every change in viewpoint. In the scene quoted above, the waitress's admiration has nothing to do with the story; all it tells us is that David is handsome and attractive to women. The author, if he had really been using the omniscient viewpoint, could have told us that directly.

If you begin a story in the single-character viewpoint, the rule is that you must stick to it. This remains true of multiple-viewpoint stories; each episode or scene must stay within one character's viewpoint. Otherwise you will wind up with something that is not omniscient, not single-character, not multiple-character, but simply a collection of mistakes.

Imagine that you are writing a story in single-character viewpoint, third person subjective. Your viewpoint character is A. Which of the following lines could be part of that story if written about characters *other than* A? (Answers below.)

1. A smile crossed her face.
2. Her eyes wavered.
3. Her hands trembled.
4. A blush warmed her cheeks.
5. He was afraid to touch it.
6. He reached for it awkwardly.
7. His hand shook as he reached for it.

Answers: 1, 2, 3, 6, 7. Numbers 1 and 2 are clearly objective. Number 3 could be either subjective or objective, and so could numbers 6 and 7. Numbers 4 and 5 are entirely subjective—they could not be observed from the outside—and therefore, if written about a character other than the viewpoint character, they would be viewpoint switches.

Remember that if you are writing from the viewpoint of a single character, you must not reveal anything that could be known only by another character. (The viewpoint character can *see* that another character is blushing, but unless he is close enough to touch her, he can't feel the warmth of the blush. When you tell us about it, you inadvertently zap us for an instant into the second character's mind—a viewpoint switch.)

Suppose there are two characters in your story, Randolph and Cynthia. Randolph is your viewpoint character. You can tell the reader anything that happens on the outside of Cynthia and the inside of Randolph, but not the other way around.

"What?" Randolph's eyes were glazed with shock. [Who sees this? Randolph can't.]
"You heard me." Cynthia was playing for time. [Randolph doesn't know this. Cynthia does, and you do, but neither one of you is allowed to speak.]

To convey the same information without leaving the viewpoint character's mind, you might write:

"What?" A shock went through his body.
"You heard me." Cynthia smiled faintly, looking down at the table. She was playing for time, he thought suddenly.

Here is a chart that may help you sort out the differences among the various viewpoints. It shows, for example, that in the omniscient viewpoint you can describe the central character and other characters as seen from the inside and the outside, whereas in single-character objective you can describe any character, whether central or not, only from the outside.

You will notice that in one respect the single-character subjective viewpoint is the most flexible of all—it can be used with first, second, or third person.

Single-character objective is rare in the first and second persons. The story about the mountain cabin, if written in the second person as I suggested, would have been in second-person objective. Dashiell Hammett's *The Thin Man,* a tour de force, is written entirely in first-person objective: the story is narrated by the viewpoint character, but he never tells us what he is thinking or feeling—only what he and others say and do.

	Central character		Other characters		Person		
	Seen from:				**Person**		
	Inside	Outside	Inside	Outside	1st	2nd	3rd
Omniscient	[ ]	[ ]	[ ]	[ ]	[*]		[ ]
Limited omniscient	[ ]	[ ]		[ ]			[ ]
Detached		[ ]		[ ]			[ ]
Single-Character Subjective	[ ]		[ ]	[ ]	[ ]	[ ]	[ ]
Single-Character Objective		[ ]		[ ]	[*]	[*]	[ ]
Multiple Character	[ ]	[ ]	[ ]	[ ]	[ ]		[ ]

*rare

Mixed Viewpoints

My aim in this book is to describe what really happens, as distinct from what teachers of writing say ought to happen, and I distrust all these categories even when I invent them myself. The categories are all right as far as they go, but they are too precise and too simple. What really happens in a story is much more complex, trickier, and subtler.

My story "Masks" is about a cyborg, a man who has had his entire body replaced by prosthetic devices. He has a secret that is not revealed until the end, and for that reason I didn't want to tell the story entirely from his subjective point of view. The story begins in the detached viewpoint; as you read, you are not linked to any one character, you are simply there, an invisible witness. Three characters are present in the first scene—Roberts, the technician, who will never appear again; Babcock, the project director, an important character; and Sinescu, the visitor from Washington, who will be gone after a few more pages. The detached viewpoint, which some critics call "camera eye" (but what kind of camera is it that can't even see people's faces?), follows Babcock and Sinescu into the elevator, where for an instant we are in Babcock's viewpoint—dizzy with fatigue, he hears only the last part of something Sinescu says to him.

Inside the cyborg's living quarters, for all we can tell we are still in the detached viewpoint, and it is only when we reach the lines, "His grip was firm and warm," and ". . . when Sinescu looked more closely, he saw that the right one was a slightly different color, not quite authentic," that we know for certain we are seeing with Sinescu's eyes and feeling with his hands. (The earlier line, "bookshelves that Sinescu fingered curiously as he passed," could be from either the detached viewpoint or Sinescu's.) The rest of this passage, until Sinescu leaves, is entirely in his viewpoint, the next one is in Babcock's, and the final section is in the cyborg's.

Let's look at another example, John O'Hara's "I Spend My Days in Longing":

It was bad enough to feel lousy when you knew what was wrong with you, but none of the doctors he had seen could

find anything wrong—organically, at least. The lungs, okay;
the ticker, okay. Go easy on the cigarettes and coffee, they
said. Be better if he did not drink so much brandy. But they
were just whistling "Dixie," and they knew it and he knew it.

We don't know this person's name yet, but we know whose
viewpoint we are in. Then we get a conversation with a doctor, remembered by the central character, and then, introduced in just the
same way, a conversation with a friend. After half a page of this it
begins to dawn on us not only that we are in the present time of the
story, but that we are not in the central character's viewpoint anymore: we are in a floating, detached viewpoint, or maybe even that
term won't do, because we are not *seeing* anything unless we invent it ourselves, only hearing what the two characters say. What
are you going to call that, a hearpoint?

Notice that in each of these stories there is a passage where the
reader *can't tell* what viewpoint she's in, and that these ambiguous
passages are there for a reason: they accomplish a change in viewpoints so subtly that it has happened before the reader knows it. (In
O'Hara's story, the ambiguous passage accomplishes a time change
as well.)

By now you may think you can do whatever you want to with
viewpoints, and the categories be damned—and you can, if you
know what you're doing. If you write without understanding the categories, you will be like an amateur painter daubing colors at random, and you will have to hide the result in a garage, or give it to
a relative you don't like.

Person

When we talk about the "person" of the story we simply mean that
the central character is referred to as *I* (first person), *you* (second
person), *he,* or *she* (third person). Notice that only in third person
is the sex of the central character made evident by the pronouns—
in first or second person, it must be established in other ways.

First person is the most intimate and direct, and many people
find it the most natural to use, but it is a trap for many young writ-

ers because they unconsciously assume it will make characterization easy. Nothing could be further from the truth. How do you let the reader know what your viewpoint character looks like? By having her look in a mirror? That one still slips by a drowsing editor once in a while, but not very often. How do you let the reader know the character's real nature, as distinct from the image she wants the world to see? All this information, which can be conveyed directly and without any fuss in third person, has to be conveyed by indirection in first person.

As if this were not enough, it is terribly hard for a young writer to separate the "I" of the story from his own "I," and that makes a whole series of new problems. Before the age of thirty or so, many people have great difficulty in admitting to themselves that they have any faults. Transfer this to a first-person character, and you get a self-admiring plaster saint. Or, if the author has the contrary set of feelings about herself, what you get is an orgy of self-contempt and self-hatred.

Finally, a first-person character assumes the role of the author of the story, and with it a third kind of difficulty. Why should we trust this person *as author*? (Or if we can't, how can we read between the lines to find out what is really happening and what the character is really like?)

There are some situations in which first person is the method of choice:

• When you want the narrator to speak directly to the readers, as in *Moby Dick*. ("Call me Ishmael.")

• When you want to give the story the flavor of a memoir, as in Stevenson's *Treasure Island*.

• When you want the narrator to conceal part of the truth, or even lie about it, as in *The Good Soldier,* by Ford Madox Ford:

"Poor dear Florence," for about a hundred pages, and then, "I hate Florence." (A first-person narrator can lie with impunity, whereas in third person it's the author who lies, and readers will resent that fiercely. Notice also that if the first-person narrator lies or conceals the truth, eventually you must allow the reader to find that out.)

If you have been using first person habitually, try translating one of your stories into third person by changing all the pronouns. Does the character seem to disappear? If so, it probably means you have been using first person as a substitute for building a character.

Most first-person stories are written in formal English and hover somewhere between a written record and a spoken narrative. (A few tip definitely one way or the other.) If the central character is a speaker of substandard or regional English, however, the story can be told in formal English only if it is put into third person.

In second-person narration, the central character is referred to as *you* rather than *I, he,* or *she:* "You were seventeen. You got up one morning and found a note under your door from your parents," etc. Second-person narration is a somewhat unnatural way of telling a story, and it is seldom used. It does have one advantage: the word *you* implies, more strongly than *he* or *she* does, the existence of an *I* who tells the story, so that, in effect, you can get two viewpoints for the price of one.

An Exercise in Viewpoint and Person

Suppose you come home one day to find that someone in your household has cut something out of the newspaper, leaving only part of a front-page story. From what is left you can tell that someone has planted a bomb in a nuclear power plant. You don't know who, why, or where; you don't know if the bomb went off or whether it was discovered in time.

Here is the raw material for a story—but what story? Whose story will it be? From whose viewpoint will it be told? The viewpoint character may be the bomber, or a technician, or the plant security officer. There are other possible choices, but looking at these three alone, we can see that each one would lead to a different story.

By choosing a viewpoint character, obviously, you choose which story to tell; or by choosing which story to tell, you choose a viewpoint character.

What is less obvious is that the story you will tell depends not only on the character but on the viewpoint and the person you choose. Omniscient, limited omniscient, detached, single-character, multiple? First, second, or third person? Subjective or objective?

Choose one of the three characters—the bomber, the technician, or the security officer—as your viewpoint character. Now pick a scene where all three are present, and write it briefly from *each* of the following viewpoints:

- limited omniscient
- first-person subjective
- third-person subjective
- third-person objective

Now choose another character, and do it again. (I could tell you in advance what you will find out by doing this exercise, but I don't want to spoil your pleasure of discovery.)

Tense

Tense, for our purposes, describes the way verbs change to show that they refer to things happening in the future, the present, or the past.

Most English texts, fiction and nonfiction, prose and poetry, are written in the past tense. This is true even though the passage you are now reading is written in present tense, and even though many people fall naturally into present tense when recounting some experience to friends: "I'm walking along the street, minding my own business, when this maniac comes up to me . . ." Present tense offers a trivial saving in time and effort in speaking—the verbs are a little easier to pronounce—but it offers no such benefit in writing. Occasional stories demand present-tense narration, or at least are the better for it—when an effect of immediacy or timelessness is wanted, for instance, or for plot purposes, as when the world is destroyed at the end of the story.

Like second-person narration, the present tense in third person seems to imply the existence of an invisible observer, a little more strongly than past tense does: "Martin walks down the gravel path between the house and the fence. He opens the mailbox, looks inside, closes it again." Here we are not inside Martin's head, as we would tend to be in past tense ("Martin walked down the gravel path," etc.); instead, we seem to be looking at him from a little distance.

Please notice that when you are writing in the past tense ("Jane walked down the street"), the *past-tense* verbs describe what is happening in the *present time* of the story; therefore, the past perfect must be used to describe anything that has happened earlier. ("Jane walked down the street where she *had seen* the accident yesterday.")

It often happens that the writer wants to describe something that has taken place before the time of the story, at such length that it would be awkward to do it all in past perfect. In these cases it is understood that the writer can start out with a sentence or two in past perfect and then switch unobtrusively to simple past:

> He had waited for half an hour, stamping his feet in the cold and smoking one cigarette after another. Finally he saw her approaching.
> "I'm sorry I'm late," she said.

[And so on; the rest of the passage is in simple past, and most readers will not even notice.]

When the narrative is in past tense, the reader and the author remain in present time, and therefore any statement in present tense, unless attributed to a character, will be taken as a comment by the author. (Such comments are called "author intrusions.")

> Sally carried the peas over to the window to shell them. The days are long when there is no one to talk to.

The author means this as Sally's thought, but it doesn't come across that way. Written in past tense, it would have been clear.

Part 4

Controlling a Story

"If I May Have Your Attention, Please—"

A writer is like a stage magician—everything he does is illusion, deception, a trick. And yet at the heart of all this theatrical illusion there is a real magic.

The real magic is a gift; it comes doubtfully, slowly, and after long effort. Nobody can tell you how to make it come. But the stage magic is something you can learn. That's why, even though the real magic is the most important thing, this book concentrates on the *techniques* of fiction—the techniques of deception, illusion, and trickery.

Whether you realize it or not, when you are in a stage magician's audience you are not just a passive spectator but a part of the performance. The magician is in control of your reactions: he makes you tense with anticipation, he makes you relax, he makes you laugh; he even controls what you see and believe.

When you read a story by a good writer, the same thing happens: your reactions are controlled; you become part of the story.

The stage magician creates his illusions partly by technical means—sleight-of-hand and mechanical devices—and partly by inducing a sort of trance state in his audience. He does this in four ways.

1. He takes advantage of the audience's *expectation of being dominated.*

2. He exhibits *a commanding presence.*

3. He gives the audience *a focus for its attention.*

4. He holds the audience's attention by various means, including the *rhythms of his speech and movement.*

As a writer, you will learn to capture your audience and make it receptive in the same four ways. Look at the list again:

143

1. The expectation of being dominated. The reader brings this expectation with her, just as the member of the magician's audience does. It is strongest when the writer is well known, but even an unknown writer acquires some status merely by being published in a book or a national magazine. Moreover, it is no accident that a story set in type is more impressive than the same story in manuscript; the publishers have done all they can to bring this about by the choice of typefaces, the design of the page, the illustrations if there are any, and so on.

2. A commanding presence. Since you, the author, are not visible to the reader, this has to take the form of an *assumption of authority.* It shows itself in the way you approach the reader—not hesitantly or timidly, expecting to be rebuffed, but confidently and decisively. By approaching in this way and by showing other immediate signs of competence, you give the reader the comfortable feeling that she is in good hands; the result is that she relaxes and lowers her resistance.

3. A focus for attention. This can be a vivid image, a description, a bit of dialogue, almost anything, but the opening paragraphs are focused on that one thing.

4. Rhythms of speech and movement. First, your sentences are fluent; one flows into the next. (If they are disjointed, the reader's attention will wander and you will lose her.) Second, the physical movement described in the story, or the movement of the imaginary camera, is also fluent and sequential.

Readers absorbed in a work of fiction really are in a sort of trance state in which time is suspended and they lose awareness of their physical surroundings. When you speak of such an experience, what do you say? "I couldn't put it down." "I was caught up in it."

The writer has put you into this quasi-hypnotic state deliberately and for good reasons: first, when you are in it, you are much more suggestible than you normally are and the writer can give you much more vivid impressions; and second, because of your suggestibility in this state, the writer can make it hard for you to stop reading. (If you stop reading, her story has failed.)

It should go without saying that if the writer is awkward she will be unable to put you into this quasi-hypnotic state, or if she does, she will jolt you out of it again, like a stage magician who drops his cards and whose rabbits don't appear. Also, it should be obvious that you will resist the trance state and break the spell unless the writer offers you a series of interesting and pleasant experiences. But if she does, you will sit waiting eagerly for the next marvelous thing, your attention focused exactly where the writer wants it to be, forgetting where you are and who you are, forgetting your job, your father-in-law, and even your physical aches and pains.

Notice the lulling, soothing quality of most good writers' prose; notice the long rhythms and the repetitions of sounds that hold your attention. These are hypnotic techniques. Other writers may capture your attention by a sudden violent sentence. "Put down that wrench!" And that's hypnotic too. (One of the earliest mesmerists, the Abbé Faria, used to put his subjects into trance by shouting, "Sleep!")

However you do it, it is important to lead the reader into the story and get him deeply involved in it before he quite knows what has happened. At the beginning, the reader has the sensation of entering the world of the story; very soon, if the writer knows her business, the story gently closes behind the reader; now he is inside, like a fly in a pitcher plant. From here on, the only problem is to hold the reader's interest and to avoid anything that would shock him out of his suspension of disbelief.

If you show your work to friends, or if you are fortunate enough to attend a good writers' conference, you will probably find that you almost never get a unanimous reaction to any story. At first you may explain this by saying that your friends and fellow students are thickheaded (especially those who dislike your work or don't understand it). In fact, there is another reason: there is no such thing as *a* story. The words on paper are only instructions used by each reader to create a story. The story itself exists in the reader's mind and nowhere else. And it is different for each reader, because no two people have the same experience, background, training, interests, and so on.

Suppose the story is about the death of a child's dog. Did the reader ever have a dog? Did she ever have a dog that died? Does she like dogs or detest them? Does she like *children*? All these things will influence her reaction to the story.

> She pushed the door open, hearing the bell clatter, and went into the dimness of the store. A gray-haired man was behind the counter.

If the reader has ever been in a country store, that brief passage will stimulate memories—but what kind of memories? Pleasant or unpleasant? Deep South or New England?

> He pushed his face nearer, so near that she found herself staring into one bloodshot eye and smelling the whiskey reek of his breath.

If the reader has ever been closer to an aggressive drunk than she wanted to be, that memory will be stimulated here, and certain emotions will come with it—different ones for each reader. Simple distaste? Disgust? Alarm? Panic? This will color the story too.

- a dusty street
- a rain-wet alley at night
- a crowded waiting room

These are all outlines for the reader to fill in with remembered colors and smells and emotions. Every story is made up of such outlines. This explains why the most popular novelists are those who appeal to the lowest common denominator among their readers, and it also explains why there is no universally admired work of fiction. There are readers who don't like Stephen King, just as there are readers who don't like Shakespeare.

The point of all this is that every time you select a topic or express an attitude, you are increasing the story's interest for some readers and decreasing it for others. A story about first-century Britain, for instance, if it is thick with authentic detail, may be *intensely* interesting to a few thousand people and absolutely boring to everybody else.

If you leave out the technical detail and archaic language, you may make the story accessible to a larger number of readers, but at the same time you will disappoint the small group. You must decide what audience you want to write for. If you choose the small group, don't complain because so few people read your stories.

One more point: Editors are paid to represent the tastes and attitudes of their readers, and sometimes they do so very successfully, but editors, like everybody else, have individual tastes, preferences, and blind spots. If your story comes back with an angry or indifferent rejection from an editor, that may be because the story is bad, or because that editor was not equipped to appreciate it. Send it out again.

On Being Interesting

A story, we say, ought to be interesting: but interesting to whom? The TV series *The Honeymooners* was interesting to millions of viewers, but not to a friend of mine who told me he got enough marital bickering at home without watching it on the tube. The movie *Alien* was interesting, but not to another friend of mine, a Vietnam veteran who had seen all the gore he ever wanted to see.

Some beginning writers assume that certain characters are interesting *ex officio:* sea captains are interesting, international spies are interesting, movie stars are interesting, housewives are not interesting. The result is that these writers don't put anything inside their characters to make them interesting, because they are presumed to be interesting in the first place. But if you put something interesting inside, even a stock clerk is interesting, and if you don't, even an ambassador isn't.

The best way to make sure that your story will interest *somebody* is to be interested in it yourself. At some time you may have had a teacher who knew an amazing amount about her subject and whose enthusiasm for it was such that she could make you feel it too. None of my teachers were like that, but I believe they exist, and I know from reading the works of John McPhee that a writer who is passionately interested and informed can make any subject fascinating to me. For another example, read the novel *Birdy* by

William Wharton. Large parts of this book are about canaries. I read these parts with absorption, and I am grateful to Wharton for making me see the universe of complexity and order in something I had thought was simple and dull.

Notice that it isn't enough to be interested *or* informed; it takes both. If you are interested in your subject but know little about it, you can't satisfy the curiosity you arouse. If you know a great deal about the subject but are not passionately interested in it (like some scientists and teachers), you will put people to sleep.

Almost every subject on first inspection looks uninteresting because it seems meaningless—just a jumble of unorganized or undifferentiated facts. Only when you have learned enough about the subject to begin to see the patterns in it can you realize how fascinating it is. The bigger the patterns, the more they include, and the easier it becomes to fit other facts into them.

Meaning, in the sense I have been using, is organized, patterned information. I believe it is true that if you yourself are fascinated enough by any subject to get deeply into it and find out what it looks like close-up, you can make it interesting to other people. The chief handicap of most young writers, aside from lack of skill, is that they don't know or understand enough about *anything.* If you are an exception, if you have gone deeply into amateur rocketry or bee-keeping, or, I don't care, even baseball or rock music, you are very lucky. If not, you should be on the alert to follow up any flicker of interest in a new subject. Don't feel it is pointless to study something that seems to have no direct relationship to what you're writing; no passionate involvement is ever entirely wasted.

I went through a period in my thirties when I was reading every book of Jung's that I could get hold of, and every book about mythology and symbolism in literature. Some of this turned up explicitly in my fiction, for instance in "The Dying Man," which could not have been written without it, but that's not what I chiefly value it for; I think it gave me a better understanding of what the universe and human beings are all about.

Recently I had a stack of books about the early Christian church beside my chair, and a friend asked me if I was reading all that just because I was interested, or was it for my writing? I told her, "Both," and that's the way I think it should be. One of the great rewards of a writer's life is that it lets you read all the books you want to without feeling guilty.

Information

Consider this sequence of statements:

The capital of the United States is Washington, DC. The Earth goes around the Sun. Two and two are four. Many disease symptoms are caused, not by bacterial toxins, but by the body's own defense system. Many young people want to go to Hollywood and become film stars. The price of beef is high. Dr. Spock's mother believed bananas were bad for children. *A* is the first letter of the alphabet.

All these statements are true, as far as I know, but they are not all equally interesting. Did you notice, as you read, that your attention quickened in at least one place, maybe two, but that your eyes tended to glaze in between? That's because a statement that tells you something new is *information;* a statement that tells you nothing new is not information, it's *noise.* If your story tells the reader nothing she doesn't know already, it is noise. Therefore you should avoid making general statements about characters, because if they are true we know them already. The particular things that make your character an individual, distinct from all others like him, are new to us—they are information. For the same reason, you should avoid repeating yourself unnecessarily—if you've told us once, we know it, and the second time you tell us it isn't information. (Remember that I said "unnecessarily." If some apparently minor item of information is going to be important later, in the resolution of the conflict, for instance, you should be careful to bring it up more than once; otherwise the reader may have forgotten it or have attached no significance to it, and the ending won't work.)

If the automatic counter in the reader's head is clicking over several times a page—"I didn't know that, I didn't know that, I didn't know that"—you will probably hold her attention. If the counter never clicks at all, you probably won't get her attention in the first place.

Authentic-sounding details of an occupation, a real place, etc., will help increase the information density of your prose—a sea story full of bulkheads and mainbraces, or a story about a plant nursery that shows us cuttings and root-balls. You may not have thought much about this kind of factual information, since you are writing about imaginary events and people, but there are several good reasons for mingling fact and fiction in this way. Factual information satisfies the reader's curiosity in itself, and it also helps create the illusion that your story is taking place in the real world. Besides that, it gives the reader confidence that you know what you're writing about. (If there is none of this in a story that clearly calls for it, she may suspect that you don't.)

Focus

This may seem paradoxical, but the first step toward achieving the sharp focus you need in fiction is to *widen* the field of your attention. If you are like most people, there have been many times recently when you walked two or three blocks without being aware of anything around you but the pavement, an occasional lamppost, a curb, another pedestrian who was in your way, and even these you saw only as vague, general shapes. You could not describe the people you passed, or the shop windows, or anything that was in your field of vision. You were focused so tightly inside yourself, preoccupied with some worry or problem or just a general dissatisfaction, that you couldn't see anything else.

Unless you are careful, the same thing may happen to you when you set out to write a story. You will know, let's say, that your central character is a young man, recently married, whose wife is quarrelsome and doesn't understand him. And you think that's enough; so you start writing the story, and you wonder why the characters don't come to life and the background never becomes clear.

Widen your field of attention. What does this young man look like? Where is he in the room, and what kind of room is it? What does his wife look like, and where is she at this moment? What time of year is it, and what time of day?

Imagine yourself as a floating camera that can drift high above the city and see it all at once, or drop lower and follow a street, look through a window, go into a house, a room—and here's your character again, but now you know a little more about him because you know where he is.

Now do it again, and this time go back through time. Where was this person when he was five? What does he remember about his first day in school? Did he have any early experience with doctors or hospitals? When and how did he discover sex? How many affairs or marriages has he had before this one? What jobs has he had, and what are his ambitions, if any? What are his likes and dislikes, his prejudices—what is likable about him? And what about his wife? Where was *she* at five, and so on, and so on?

Now, when you come back to the room, you know much more about both the husband and the wife, so much more that when you focus closely on them, they will be doing and saying things that express their individual natures. The focus will be sharp, not because it is narrow, but because it is *specific*.

Compression

Madame de Staël once wrote, "If I had more time, I should have written you a shorter letter." She meant, of course, that she was working out what she wanted to say as she went along, instead of thinking it through and then saying it briefly. If you are writing short stories this way, they are probably running to seven and eight and ten thousand words, and editors are probably sending them back. Compression is a matter of planning and method—like packing things carefully in a suitcase instead of throwing them in all anyhow.

Suppose your story is about two young women who share an apartment. You begin by describing them and their relationship, and when you have finished doing so you discover that you have written six pages in which nothing has happened. You were inventing and exploring the characters as you wrote, instead of inventing them first and writing afterward. But the effort may not have been wasted. Now that you know the characters, put that beginning aside and write another one, focusing on some significant event or action. If you really do know your characters by this time, everything of value in the first version will be present in the second, but in a compressed form. Probably you will find that many things you wrote out in full, including long dialogues between the two characters, should have been treated as narrative summaries—e.g., "One evening they argued for an hour about whether a tomato was a fruit or a vegetable."

Before you begin your next short story, make a list of the scenes and episodes in it, and write down the number of pages you think each one will need. Now you have a series of compartments into which you will pack your story. If the total tells you that the story will be more than six thousand words long, go back over the list and reduce the number of pages. When you have written the first scene or episode, if it is spilling over its compartment, you are either going to have to reduce it somehow, or else trim down another section to make room for it.

Look at the scenes or episodes that make up your story. Are any of them unnecessary? Out with them. Have any necessary sections been omitted? (For instance, have you forgotten to establish some fact that is needed to make the ending believable?) What is each section intended to do? Is there anything in that section that does not contribute toward its principal function, or that actively works against it? (For instance, by explaining too much too soon, does the opening destroy the suspense it should be creating?)

In a short story, every scene must contribute to the pattern. If any scene or incident, or even any word or sentence, has no function, it must be pruned. In fact, the problem of compression in a short story is so acute that every passage must perform three or four functions at the same time—advance the plot, add to the characterizations, introduce background information, and so on—like a juggler keeping three or four balls in the air at once.

If you are having trouble with this, try listing in advance everything that you want to accomplish in each scene. First determine what the main purpose of the scene is. (If it has none that you can find, maybe the scene doesn't belong in the story.) Then ask yourself *what else* the scene can be used for. Will it carry more information if you move it from one location to another? Introduce an additional character? Make something else happen that will strengthen the plot, or add to the background, or reveal character?

This really is a little easier than it sounds. To begin with, your scene will probably begin when something happens, or, even better, when something is about to happen. Your characters are there, they are reacting to the thing that is happening or about to happen, and in the process we learn something about them (characterization). The thing that is happening is happening in some specific place, and we see that too (setting). As the characters talk, we learn something about where they came from and how they got where they are (background). All the opportunities are there; the only trick is to remember to use them.

An Exercise in Compression

Choose a published story that you like and go through the first page or so with a set of colored pens. Mark the parts that tell you something about the characters with one color; the parts that develop the plot with another; the parts that convey setting with another, and so on. Notice how many times two or more colors overlap.

Now do the same thing with one of your own stories. Compare the two. Do the colors overlap as much in your story as in the other? If not, you see where your problem is. Look again at each sentence that performs only one function. Is it a sentence that *tells* the reader something? Try making it *show* instead.

The Advantage of Surprise

It would be hard to overrate the value of surprise in fiction. The ending of a story is almost always a surprise of some kind, and very often the beginning is too. Here is the opening of a story by John Collier that surprised and delighted me:

> There are certain people who do not come to full flower until they are well over fifty. Among these are all males named Murchison.

Within a story, there are surprises in the ways people speak and act, and even in individual sentences there are surprises of diction.

An Exercise in Surprise

Take a scene from one of your own stories in which two people are saying exactly what anyone would expect them to. Rewrite, asking yourself, "What could they say that would be *surprising*?"

Don't take the easy way out and make them say something bizarre and irrelevant. Everything a character says should tell us something about that character, preferably something we didn't know before.

In Coward's play *Blithe Spirit,* for instance, Charles Condomine and his wife have an awkward new maid; the old one had to leave because she was pregnant. Charles says about the new one, "Perhaps we ought to keep her in more." This is surprising; it is also witty and rather cruel, exactly in keeping with Charles's character.

Pleasures Like Beads on a String

The other day, at the desk of the public library, I noticed a skinny, intense-looking boy of about twelve with a stack of books so tall that he could barely get his chin over it; and for a moment I was twelve again. I remembered exactly how it felt to have a stack of books like that in my hands, their weight against my chest, their wonderful dusty smell in my nostrils.

When I was a child I tunneled through the public library like a shipworm. Whenever I found a book of a kind I liked or by an author I liked, I read all the other books of that kind or by that author that I could find on the shelves. I read novels about knights in armor, pirate stories, mysteries; I read the works of Mary Roberts Rinehart, Rafael Sabatini, Charles Dickens, Alexandre Dumas, Edgar Allan Poe, Hugh Walpole. When these veins pinched out, I took random samples of the novels on the shelves, and in that way made new discoveries. I read only for pleasure—more precisely, for delight; I never read a book because I had been told I ought to.

Surely everybody who seriously wants to be a writer has had this experience of books, and yet beginning writers often seem to forget that reading is pleasure. I think what sometimes happens is that we start out writing frivolous things; then we notice that published fiction is not like that, and we turn out stories that are increasingly earnest and grim.

Reading a story, even a tragic story, ought to be a succession of sweet pleasures, like beads on a string—vivid images, excitements, anticipations, surprises. "Serious" doesn't have to mean dismal. Even if a story *is* dismal, it doesn't have to be dismal *all the way through.*

One almost universal fault of beginners' fiction is that it lacks contrast. Any photography student or beginning musician would know what I mean by this word, but it seldom occurs to beginning writers that if a story strikes only one note, over and over, it may be a great note, but the story will still be monotonous.

Make a list of things you love, that give you intense pleasure just to look at them or smell or taste them. Now look at your grim story. How many things like that does it evoke? There ought to be at least one. (Read "One Day in the Life of Ivan Denisovich," by Alexander Solzhenitsyn, or "A Perfect Day for Bananafish," by J. D. Salinger.)

Voice and Persona

Voice is the distinctive pattern that makes a writer's work recognizable. It is not, as a rule, the same pattern that the author uses in speaking, although it may give that impression. More often, it is the characteristic voice of the writer's persona.

When I was about forty I experienced a sort of leap of confidence and capability; I was writing much more freely and productively, and I was writing much better than I ever had before. After a while I realized what I had done: I had invented an imaginary writer to write my stories for me, someone who was much more mature, more skilled, more inventive, and more knowledgeable than I was. It wasn't until years later that I found out that other people knew about this and that there was a name for it: *persona,* which is Greek for "mask"—the sort of mask that Greek actors wore, putting on a role and a head at the same time.

Since then I have found myself adopting new personae several times: once when I began writing critical essays, for instance, and again when I wrote this book. The sample passages from imaginary stories (the two versions of the story about James Maxwell, for instance) were written by still another persona; they are not at all like my own fiction.

You may well ask, how can you invent a writer who can write better than you do? It would be a sophistry for me to reply with another question, such as, how can you invent a character who does things you have never done?

I don't know if you will like this any better, but I am about half convinced that when you use a persona you are drawing on the ability you will develop much later—borrowing against future earnings. The other half of the time I think this is nonsense and that what you are doing when you call up a persona to write for you is just to make a greater demand on the creative powers of your unconscious.

Another way to look at it is this: Suppose that in the course of a long story you find that you need to include a passage from an imaginary work by one of the characters in the story. Obviously that passage must be written by a different persona, because the character is not you. If you can do that in a brief excerpt, why not in a whole story?

An Exercise in Voice and Persona

A young woman and a young man are walking with their arms around each other. She rests her hand casually on his buttock.

Invent a writer who finds this scene healthful and innocent, and let him describe it as he would in a story.

Invent another writer who considers the scene disgusting and immoral; again, let him describe it in a scene from a story. Use the detached viewpoint in both passages.

When you have done this successfully, in such a way that the writer's attitude is fully evident, in each passage, just from an apparently objective description of the scene, you will realize that you could in fact write a whole story *as if* it were written by either of these people. You have just invented two personae.

Tone and Mood

Tone in fiction is like the tone of a storyteller's voice: is it playful, serious, melancholy, frightening, or what? (It can be any of these things, and still be the same voice.)

Mood has to do with the emotions the author makes the reader feel in less direct ways—by the sounds of the words she uses, the length and rhythm of sentences, the choice of images and their associations.

Sometimes tone and mood are most effective when they are mismatched. In the first of the two following examples, the tone is solemn and the mood is hilarious; in the second, the tone is matter-of-fact and the mood is one of horror.

In about half an hour an old gentleman, with a flowing beard and a fine but rather austere face, entered, and sat down at my invitation. He seemed to have something on his mind. He took off his hat and set it on the floor, and got out of it a red silk handkerchief and a copy of our paper.

He put the paper on his lap, and while he polished his spectacles with his handkerchief he said, "Are you the new editor?"

I said I was.

"Have you ever edited an agricultural paper before?"

"No," I said; "this is my first attempt."

"Very likely. Have you had any experience in agriculture practically?"

"No; I believe I have not."

"Some instinct told me so," said the old gentleman, putting on his spectacles, and looking over them at me with asperity, while he folded his paper into a convenient shape. "I wish to read to you what must have made me have that instinct. It was this editorial. Listen, and see if it was you that wrote it:

" 'Turnips should never be pulled, it injures them. It is much better to send a boy up and let him shake the tree.'

"Now, what do you think of that?—for I really suppose you wrote it?"

"Think of it? Why, I think it is good. I think it is sense. I have no doubt that every year millions and millions of bushels of turnips are spoiled in this township alone by being pulled in a half-ripe condition, when, if they had sent a boy up to shake the tree—"

"Shake your grandmother! Turnips don't grow on trees!"

"Oh, they don't, don't they? Well, who said they did? The language was intended to be figurative, wholly figurative. Anybody that knows anything will know that I meant that the boy should shake the vine."

"How I Edited an Agricultural Paper," by Mark Twain

It was now midnight, and my task was drawing to a close. I had completed the eighth, the ninth, and the tenth tier. I had finished a portion of the last and the eleventh; there remained but a single stone to be fitted and plastered in. I struggled with its weight; I placed it partially in its destined position. But now there came from out the niche a low laugh that erected the hairs upon my head. It was succeeded by a sad voice, which I had difficulty in recognizing as that of the noble Fortunato. The voice said—

"Ha! ha! ha!—he! he!—a very good joke indeed—an excellent jest. We will have many a rich laugh about it at the palazzo—he! he! he!—over our wine—he! he! he!"

"The Amontillado!" I said.

"He! he! he!—he! he! he!—yes, the Amontillado. But is it not getting late? Will not they be awaiting us at the palazzo, the Lady Fortunato and the rest? Let us be gone."

"Yes," I said, "let us be gone."

"For the love of God, Montresor!"

"Yes," I said, "for the love of God!"

But to these words I hearkened in vain for a reply.

"The Cask of Amontillado," by Edgar Allan Poe

An Exercise in Setting As Mood

Imagine a character who is sitting or standing, alone, in the room you are now in. See the room through his eyes; write a page or so of pure description of the room, *without mentioning the character or referring to him in any way,* but bearing in mind as you write that he has just had a phone call notifying him of a promotion and a raise. (Assume that the person lives here, if the room you are in is part of a house or apartment; if it isn't, assume that the job has something to do with this room.) How does his emotional state color his perceptions? Remember that you are not allowed to refer to the character, even by using a pronoun ("I looked at the furniture," for instance). Tell only what he sees.

Now describe the same room as seen by a person who has just had a phone call from a homicidal maniac: "I'm coming to kill you." Follow the same rules as before.

Style

Style is the visible trace of a workman solving her problems. Good style is the trace of a workman solving her problems with economy and grace, leaving her individual mark.

Don't confuse style with ornament, and don't worry about developing your own individual style. It is likely that you will have a recognizable style long before you master your tools—it just won't be a very good style. After a certain point, you will put your individual imprint on everything you do, whether you want to or not. What you need to learn is not individuality but skill.

Good prose is balanced somewhere between the straightforward, no-nonsense style of an instruction manual and the evocative, sensitive style of a poem. The trouble with most beginning writers, I think, is not that they don't know this but that they are using bad poetry as their model. Poetry to a high-school student is usually greeting-card verse.

I said earlier that you ought to read widely in fiction, just in order to know what has been done and what traditions you have to work with. Now I want to tell you that you should read poetry too, for the same reason. If you are wise you will also write it—not free verse, at least to begin with, but rhymed, metric poems—sonnets, triolets, even limericks. Working within the constraints of formal verse will strengthen your grasp of prose.

If you have never tried this before, you will need a good book on prosody. The one I used years ago was Burges Johnson's *Rhyming Dictionary;* the one I have now is Judson Jerome's *The Poet's Handbook.* Look up *foot* and *meter* first, then *sonnet,* or whatever form you want to try. (Jerome's book is a delight to read; if you were turned off poetry in high school, as I was, it may turn you on again.)

Six Ways to Think about Style

1. Variety (of sentence structure, length; of sounds, of rhythm). The most common stylistic error of beginning writers is to repeat the same sentence structure again and again, usually a simple declarative sentence: "Jack got out of bed. He got dressed. He put some coffee on," etc.

An Exercise in Variety

Find a passage in one of your own stories in which, for five or six sentences, the subject is always in the same place—either at the beginning, as in the example above, or in the middle, as in the following example: "No matter how he tried, he could not seem to get out of debt. Even though he scrimped and saved, they were always further behind at the end of the month. As Father had always said, 'A fool and his money are soon parted.' " Revise, making sure that the subject does not appear in the same place in more than two consecutive sentences.

2. Fluency. Any fault—a misplaced word, a wrong word, an ugly repetition of sounds, a needlessly complicated sentence—can interrupt the *flow* of your narrative and make the reader stumble. This topic overlaps "economy and clarity," below—the examples given there are awkward, unfluent. Fluency is important, not just for esthetic reasons, but because it is one of the devices that draw the reader into the story.

3. Consecutiveness is another of these devices. If your writing is both fluent and consecutive—that is, if one sentence leads naturally into the next—you can keep a person reading almost against her will, just because there isn't any convenient place to stop.

To illustrate, here is a passage in which the phrases and sentences are out of their natural order:

> Egmont dug into the sandy soil between the clump of alders and the meadow. His pale eyes stared unblinkingly at the overturned earth. He had been digging for three-quarters of an hour and his skin was shiny with sweat. His fine yellow hair wavered in the breeze.

In this paragraph our attention is directed first to the sandy soil, then Egmont's pale eyes, then a summary statement about the length of time he has been digging, then his sweaty skin, and finally his yellow hair.

Put this passage into a natural order and see the difference:

> Egmont dug into the sandy soil between the clump of alders and the meadow. His fine yellow hair wavered in the breeze, and his skin was shiny with sweat. His pale eyes stared unblinkingly at the overturned earth. He had been digging for three-quarters of an hour.

In this version the viewpoint is like a motion-picture camera, which first gives us an overall view of the scene, then moves in to focus on the most striking detail—Egmont's yellow hair—then his sweaty skin, then (still moving closer) his pale eyes, and finally a summary statement that may be the pivot for a transition to Egmont's viewpoint.

An Exercise in Fluency and Consecutiveness

Here is another passage in which the order of the sentences has been scrambled. Try to reassemble it in its natural order.

> From the outside, the old gray house looked ancient and abandoned. The rooms were high-ceilinged, each with its Georgian mantel and bricked-up fireplace. A light rain was falling when the visitors arrived. A scurrying of rats could be heard in the wainscoting. Within, the passage was musty, but there was a carpet on the floor, not much moth-eaten. Rooks flew in and out of the holes where slates had fallen, and a tree had pushed its branches through one of the dormer windows.

4. Precision. In this brief passage there are seven grossly misused words.

> Flaunting Robert's orders, Edgar deliberately approached the flowers, admiring the bright colors of their livid blossoms. Robert watched him somberly, yawning with disinterest. He

had not even asked Edgar what had transpired during his journey, and yet it had been the most fortuitous thing that had ever happened to Edgar. The realization of what it all meant had hit him like the proverbial ton of bricks, at the moment when he had seen Gregory's decapitated head rolling on the floor. . . .

To flaunt means to display provocatively, not to defy; *livid* means pale (or blue-black, like a bruise), not vivid; *disinterest* means lack of bias, not boredom; *to transpire* means to become known, not to happen; *fortuitous* means accidental, not fortunate; *proverbial* means having to do with a proverb, not with a cliché; *decapitated* means made headless, not severed.

An Exercise in Precision

Did you know all this before I told you? If not, there is a chance that you are misusing other words. Choose a paragraph of one of your own stories that contains a fairly high proportion of long or unusual words. Now look up in the dictionary *every word* in that paragraph. (Yes, even *the.*) This test should tell you whether you have a problem or not. If you do, there is only one remedy. Use the dictionary as you read, and use it to correct your own work in first draft. If you have only a vague idea of the difference between one word and another, you are like a carpenter who has only a vague idea of the difference between a screwdriver and a corkscrew.

5. Economy. Use the smallest number of words that will say exactly what you mean. The more you clutter up your prose with unnecessary words, the less chance you have of getting any intensity of feeling or perception.

6. Clarity. Use the simplest words that will say exactly what you mean. Break yourself of any tendency to prefer long words just because they are long. Beware of vagueness, for instance a "he" that could refer to either of two people.

An Exercise in Economy and Clarity

Here are two passages of uneconomical and unclear writing. The first has been corrected. Use this as a model to correct the second one.

They got into the boat and sat down on the seats, then began using the oars, gliding with an absence of sound through the liquid medium. For several minutes Mac did not say anything to Jim; he let his breath out through his nose with a whistling sound that showed he was angry with Jim but was suppressing it. Jim did not feel comfortable at all. He was supposed to be the leader and take care of the one who was his subordinate, and here he was acting like this.

They told him at the station that nobody came back alive. They were too large, too fierce and carnivorous to fight. "They'll kil you just like the others." Howard rejected their beliefs because his self-esteem was so great that it would not permit him to listen to the dictates of other people.

They got into the boat and began rowing. The boat glided silently through the water. For a while Mac did not speak; he breathed with a whistling sound that meant he was suppressing his anger. Jim felt uncomfortable. Mac was supposed to be the leader and take care of Jim; why was he acting like this?

Note: In order to correct this passage, you will have to add information omitted by the author. Who are "they," for instance, in the first sentence? In the second?

Awkward Repetitions

Repetitions of words and sounds will creep in, and you may find it hard at first to detect them in your own work. Reading aloud often helps.

> He stretched out on the shore, shivering several times in the sunlight. His black thatch of hair was a patch of blackness against the sand. Back from the water's edge, sedges grew in the harsh wind; the marsh was full of bird cries. Clouds of flies hovered in the heavy humid air.

Some of this unintended rhyme, consonance, and alliteration is just carelessness, and some of it is Fred being reminded of one word by the sound of another. *Stretched, shivering, several,* and *sunlight* are too many sibilants too close together. Then we have *black, blackness,* and *back, thatch* and *patch, edge* and *sedges, harsh* and *marsh, cries* and *flies,* and finally a series of *h*'s.

Revised, this passage might read:

> He lay down on the shore, trembling in the sunlight. His hair was a patch of darkness against the sand. Away from the water, sedges grew in the bitter wind; the marsh was full of bird calls. Clouds of flies hovered in the humid air.

Rhyme, alliteration, and consonance (the repetition of final consonantal sounds) often appear in prose when it approaches the intensity of poetry. If you use these devices with awareness, they may be good or bad, depending on your skill. If you use them accidentally, they will almost certainly be bad.

Notice that the revised version, above, is not only more readable but shorter—it says much the same thing, but with fewer words.

The *Ing* Disease

Often when I read student stories I come across an outbreak of words that end in "ing." Here is a typical example:

> Open*ing* the door, he sprang up the creak*ing* stairway, climb*ing* as swiftly as a rocket to the sitt*ing* room where he pulled open the drawer of the writ*ing* desk and took out the glitter*ing* r*ing*.

The first of these is a misused simultaneous construction, to be avoided as a fault in itself (the hero couldn't do all that while open-ing the door, even if his arms were forty feet long). The others are a kind of echolalia, as if the first "ing" had set off some mecha-nism in the mind that likes to go "ing, ing." Train yourself to look for these. Wherever there are two "ing" words close together, you will almost always find three or four more farther down.

Negative Practice

One way to rid yourself of habitual faults of the kind we have been discussing here is just to look for them and correct them in your rough drafts. If that doesn't work, you might try a neat trick that psychologists call "negative practice." Whatever the fault is, instead of trying to avoid it as you write, deliberately commit it as often as you can. The purpose of this, bizarre as it sounds, is to turn a fault you commit unconsciously into one you are conscious of and can therefore control.

Dialogue

"Well, Rod, here we are on the planet Mars after our long ten-month voyage from Earth to carry out our important mission for the United Nations." "Yes, Don, and our first task is to make sure the rocket ship was not seriously damaged by the meteorite that struck it dur-ing our landing approach." (For some reason these people are al-ways named Rod and Don.)

"Well, you know, uh, the way I see it—look, when somebody asks a question, like, well, if they would give you some idea, but I mean hey, how do I know?"

Good dialogue falls somewhere between these two extremes. The first is wooden; the characters sound as if they're reading from cue cards. The second is what you might find in the transcript of the conversation of a not very literate or articulate person.

Dialogue in fiction should resemble real dialogue with the various hesitations, repetitions, and other glitches edited out of it. Listen to people talk. No two are exactly alike. By the way they talk, their choice of words, the things they talk about, and the attitudes they express, they tell you where they grew up, how they were educated, the kind of work they do, what social class they belong to, and much more. When you know who your character is and where she comes from and what she's like, you should know instinctively what she will say and how she'll say it. If the people in your stories *don't* talk "in character," it must be because you don't know them well enough, or because you have not spent enough time listening attentively to people's speech patterns.

Two Exercises in Dialogue

1. Think of someone you know who has a strongly individual way of speaking. Imagine her in a fictional situation, having a conversation with a character you have invented. Try to make her speech so characteristic that any friend of hers who read it could identify her.

If this doesn't work the first time, put it aside until you see your friend again. This time, listen more carefully to the way she talks. Make mental notes of any peculiarities you notice, and write them down later. Then do the exercise over.

2. Four people are in a room, relaxed and talking comfortably. Imagine them in as much detail as you like; write a brief biographical sketch of each one if you wish. If you are a woman, make them all men; if you are a man, make them women. When you are sure that you have their personalities firmly in mind and can easily tell them apart, write a page or more of dialogue without any attributions—just the words as a microphone might pick them up. Don't make it easy for yourself by having them address each other by name, or by giving them distinctive regional accents, or any such trick. Keep doing this until you are able to make it clear who is speaking at any moment.

Speech Tags

These are the phrases attached to dialogue to let the reader know who is speaking. *He said* or *she said* attached to every speech becomes tiresome, but there are five or six legitimate substitutes for it, and other ways of avoiding it gracefully. A person can mutter, whisper, shout, scream, gasp, and so on, but if there is too much of that going on in a story it begins to sound like feeding time at the zoo. *Reply, protest, point out,* and a few others are tolerable in moderation, and often no speech tag at all is necessary.

> "Do you want some coffee?" she asked.
> "No, thanks."

Since there is only one other person in the room, we know who the speaker is without being told. Beware, however, of long exchanges without any identification of speakers; after the sixth or seventh speech the reader may lose track and have to count forward from the beginning.

A common beginner's fault is to try to think of a new speech tag every time, and avoid *he said* altogether. Don't do this, and don't use tags that have nothing to do with speech:

> "Come in," she invited.

You can *say* "Come in," or whisper it, or shout it, but you can't invite it, propose it, frown it, or offer it. Equally objectionable are phrases that are not speech tags at all, but accompanying actions:

> "Come in," he buttered his toast.

Dialect

Don't try to represent any regional speech in written form unless you know it thoroughly at first hand. If you do use it, don't try to spell it phonetically:

> "Wail, hail, Beelly-Jeeyim, Ah nevah thote yeoo wuz gonna do theyat."

Instead, try to suggest the regional flavor:

> "Well, hell, Billy-Jim, I never thought you was gonna do that."

Thoughts

"I'd better not go in there," he thought.
I'd better not go in there, he thought.
I'd better not go in there, he thought.
He'd better not go in there, he thought.
He'd better not go in there.

All five of these conventions are in current use; the last three are recommended because they are simplest and do least to break the flow of a narrative in past tense. Putting the thought in quotation marks has the disadvantage of possible confusion with spoken dialogue; italics overemphasize thoughts, especially when there are a good many of them on a page.

A Cautionary Note

If you are inquiring and observant, you will probably find all the faults I discuss here in published fiction. Well, then, you will say, if so many published stories are bad according to Knight, why can't I write bad stories and get them published too? God knows. Maybe you *can*. There are markets for what I consider bad fiction, plenty of them—more paying markets than there are for fiction that I consider good. Some of these markets, maybe, print bad stories because they can't get anything better, and others actively encourage badness because it sells. (I'm talking about art, not commerce. In commercial terms, by definition, anything that sells is good.)

One problem is the matter of taste. If you don't like the kind of fiction a certain magazine publishes, you won't be able to tell the difference between the bad things the editor doesn't care about and the ones she *likes*.

Another problem is whether you can hit what you aim at. If you try to write the very best you can, you may produce something pretty good. If you try to write bad fiction, you will probably end up with something that is not merely bad but unreadable.

I wish now that I had saved specimens from the slushpiles of manuscripts I read when I was an editor. Most of these amateur efforts are foul beyond imagining, worse than anything I have told you about here. It is hard to know what goes through the minds of their authors, but maybe they are saying to themselves, "This magazine publishes bad stuff, so I can sell them bad stuff too."

Part 5

FINISHING A STORY

What to Do When You're Stuck

Halfway through a story that has been going rapidly and well, you come to a section that you can't write, for no evident reason. The sensation is a little bit like being suspended by your thumbs.

If your feeling toward the part you can't write is one of bewilderment and frustration, the trouble is probably that you have failed to consult Fred about this part—you can't write it because your conception of it is wrong, or because you don't know enough about it.

Maybe you are stopped because you haven't figured out what the next important event will be, and you're trying to build a bridge with only one end. Or maybe you have just written a sentence that leads to a blind alley. Try striking out the last sentence.

If you are stopped because one of your characters is refusing to follow the script, it may mean that you don't know enough about the character—probably does—but it can also mean that because you now know more about her than you did when you planned the story, you are trying to cram her into a box too small for her. If you persist, you will lose the plausibility of the story, and that's what Fred is trying to tell you. There are only two solutions to this: let the character do what she wants, or change the circumstances so that she will voluntarily do what *you* want.

If your feeling toward the part you can't write is one of hopeless boredom, the chances are Fred is signaling that this part ought to be drastically scaled down or eliminated. In that case, one thing you can try is to skip the troublesome part and come back to it later. You may find it wasn't necessary in the first place; then you can simply leave it out. If that doesn't work—if the section really is necessary—try getting through it as briefly as possible. You may have been thinking of it as a fully developed section three or four pages

173

long, whereas all it really needs is a couple of paragraphs. No wonder you were bored.

If you are stuck for a name, a place, a date, or something equally trivial, skip it and go on. Mark the place with a pair of virgules (//) or some other symbol to call your attention to it when you correct what you have written. If you think the word that comes to you isn't quite right, put it down anyway with a virgule on either side. Nine times out of ten, something that might hold you up for half an hour at the keyboard will solve itself in a minute or two later on.

The Ending

The ending of a story should round it off in some way, make the reader feel that the pattern is complete. Here, if anywhere, the author has a chance to make the reader understand what the whole meaning of the story is. Since (usually) the lives of the characters continue past the end of the story, often this completion of form has to be implied rather than stated.

The ending, at any rate, should satisfy the reader—should explain the mystery or solve the puzzle or whatever. Unless you have lost control of the story and have written it into a blind alley, the ending ought to be easier to write than the beginning, because it has the whole momentum of the story behind it.

Revision

When you have written the last page, you may feel drained by the effort, and in any event you will probably be too close to the story to be able to criticize it. Put it away for a day or a week, take it out again and try to look at it as if it had been written by someone else.

Does the story make sense, or mean anything to you? If it doesn't, you will have to decide whether to abandon it or rewrite it completely.

Does it hang together structurally? Are there missing pieces? Unnecessary pieces? Look carefully at the opening, particularly the first sentence. Is it comprehensible, does it convey any information? Have you answered the four questions, *who, where, what,* and *when*? Do you at least know the answer to the fifth question, *why*?—and is the opening consistent with your answer? If not, rewrite. Look at the ending. Is it really an ending, or just a fadeout? If you have left the story without an ending because you couldn't think of one, think again. (What have you left out of the early part of the story that would make an ending possible?)

The characters—are they believable and consistent? Have you used the best point of view, person, and tense for the story? If not, you must consider again whether to abandon the story or rewrite completely.

Now, assuming that you have passed all these hurdles, look at the surface of the story—make every word and phrase justify its use. If you have trouble, as many writers do, in focusing your attention on a single word or phrase, cut two L-shaped pieces of paper and arrange them to block out everything on the page except the one word or phrase you want to examine. If a sentence seems awkward, try rearranging it; in the process, you may shorten and clarify it.

Look for inadvertent changes in viewpoint and correct them. Read your dialogue aloud. Does it sound natural, unforced? Can you tell the dialogue from the narrative by its sound and rhythm? If not, rewrite.

Strike down clichés. Correct errors in spelling and syntax. If the manuscript is heavily corrected at this point, make a clean copy and then go over it carefully again. Repeat this process until you can't stand the sight of the manuscript anymore.

Writing for a Market

Writers of fiction range all the way from dedicated esthetes who publish only in little magazines to cheerful mercenaries who will turn out whatever an editor asks for. Most of us are somewhere in the middle. If you want to devote your life to the pursuit of excellence in fiction, expecting no more reward than publication in a magazine read by five or six hundred people, I don't see why not. If all you want is to make a decent living by writing things other people want to read, I think that's okay too.

It is not always possible to tell in advance which writers are going to wind up famous. James Joyce's early work was published in small editions and in little magazines; on the other hand, Georges Simenon turned out potboiling thrillers for thirty years before he was recognized as a literary artist. Any honest workman has my respect. It would be foolish for you to worry about not being some kind of writer you are not capable of being and really have no desire to be.

If you expect to be published, however, you must have some market in mind and you must know something about that market. Every short-story market has its own invisible boundaries, and they are almost never defined except by the most degraded and cynical magazines (e.g., "Stories for us must be about happy, successful women between the ages of twenty and thirty-five"). What every editor is looking for is freshness and novelty *within* her particular set of boundaries. If, in your ignorance, you send her something that is fresh and novel but falls outside those boundaries, she will send it back, probably without trying to explain why. She expects you to know where the boundaries are. If you haven't taken the trouble to find out, she doesn't see why she should waste her time on you.

The best way, and almost the only way, to find out where the boundaries are is to read a lot of stories in the magazines you hope to be published in. A casual sampling won't do. You must immerse yourself in those stories, and you had better like them or you won't be able to stand it.

Commercial fiction markets are subject to cycles and fads, as well as the disintegration into categories that has been going on since the late 1920s. The Western short story, once the largest category of popular fiction, is now almost extinct. Mysteries, horror and occult fiction, suspense stories, spy stories come and go. At the moment, the largest category of adult short fiction, in magazines and anthologies of original stories, is science fiction, followed by mysteries, family fiction, gay and lesbian fiction, women's fiction, and "quality" fiction—the kind published in the *Atlantic Monthly, Harper's,* and *The New Yorker.* All this may change radically within a few years, and in any event, you must do your own market study in order to find out anything useful.

The easiest short-story markets for a new writer to break into are the science-fiction magazines. They pay relatively poorly, they use a great many stories, and they are not fastidious about style or any other literary quality. This doesn't mean that you can't sell a good story there, but it means that even if your story is awkwardly written and superficial, it may be bought if it has a good idea entertainingly presented.

In addition to the commercial markets, there is a large and fluctuating number of literary quarterlies and "little" magazines. Some of them pay for stories; others give only a free copy or two of the issue in which a story appears. They are not markets for a writer who hopes to live by her work, but some of them are valuable as showcases; many editors read these magazines.

Most fiction writers who support themselves by their work do so by writing novels; generally speaking, novels pay better for the time invested, and they give the writer more latitude. Nevertheless, most writers begin with short stories. Writing short stories will teach you your craft and prepare you to do longer work, and it involves less risk. (If a short story doesn't sell, you've lost a week or so; if a novel doesn't sell, a year or more may have gone down the drain.)

If and when you do attempt a novel, you should research the market for it just as you would do for a short story. Find out which publishers are publishing the kind of novel yours is, and send it there.

Literary Market Place and other market guides list all U.S. trade publishers and their requirements. Writers' magazines sometimes have more recent information. From one of these sources, find out an editor's name and use it. If you're not sure which editor to write to (for instance, if you want to send a mystery novel to a company that publishes many other kinds of books), call the company and ask. A manuscript addressed to "The Editors" will be read, if at all, by the lowest person on the totem pole.

Many young writers are paralyzed by a fear of failure: if they submit a manuscript and get it back with a rejection slip, they will know they aren't good enough, but if they keep the story in a drawer, they can still dream. Other times the problem is a fear of success: the writer knows that if her stories are published, her life will be changed—her marriage, for instance, may not survive.

It really comes down to the question, How badly do you want to be a writer? I can't answer that for you. But I can tell you that nobody will break into your house, take away the manuscripts in your drawer, publish them, and send you money.

Before you send the manuscript out the first time, make a list of ten publishers. If it comes back from the first one, send it to the next, and the next, and the next. Keep track of the date of each submission. If a publisher has had a short story for six weeks, or a novel for three months, it's time for a polite query. This process is slow, but if your story or novel is publishable, the chances are that somebody, sometime, will publish it.

Three Errors to Avoid

1. Writing about what you think other people are interested in, as distinct from what interests you. This leads to falsity and slackness, and your manuscript will come back marked, "So what?" It is not enough to have discovered that your market is keenly interested in family relationships; if you supply them in your fiction without being interested in them yourself, if you *pretend* an interest, you won't fool anybody. Somewhere inside the boundaries there must be something that does interest you, something that you can write about with enthusiasm. If there really isn't, you had better look for another market.

2. Slavish imitation. Editors may seem to have a narrow set of requirements, but within those requirements they don't want the same old thing, they want something new. A good friend of mine, an accomplished science-fiction writer, once spent two months reading spy novels and analyzing them to find out what the required structure was (he discovered, for instance, that the hero's best friend has to die in chapter 7). He wrote an outline faithfully incorporat-

ing all these elements, but nobody would have it—it was "too familiar."

3. Writing about characters who are not interested in *themselves* but are just going through the motions—bored, apathetic, self-pitying, passive, and so on. This may be an expression of resentment on the writer's part at being forced to write about people and events he thinks are dull; but it is the wrong expression. Nearly every category market, no matter how stereotyped, will tolerate some writers who are irreverent toward its icons—who write about cowardly gunslingers, or incompetent detectives, or happy adulterers.

Dealing with Editors

For most writers the turning point comes when editors stop sending printed rejection slips and begin writing personal notes. At first these may be entirely uninformative: "Not quite," or "Try again." Later they may become a little more explicit, but probably not much, and the writer will have to try to figure out what it was that the editor disliked (even though the editor himself may not have been sure). If the comment says, for instance, "I rather liked this but thought the ending was a disappointment," it is up to the writer to decide if there really is anything wrong with the ending, and if so, to find some way of making it stronger. (Sometimes the ending is all right in itself but it hasn't been properly prepared for—it's the beginning, not the end, that needs work.)

Once in a great while the editor may say, "If this were shorter, I could buy it." Cut the story as requested, even if the editor has asked you to cut it in half. In order to do this, you will have to examine every scene, then every paragraph, then every sentence, then every phrase, and at last every word, to see whether the story can do without it. You will bleed copiously, but the experience will do you more good than a dozen lectures.

An Exercise in Cutting

Don't wait for an editor to ask you. Choose a short-story manuscript, preferably one longer than six thousand words, and cut
it by one-quarter, using the methods described above.

Part 6

BEING A WRITER

Your Byline

Choose it carefully, because once you have been published under it you may be stuck with it. Avoid anything that looks like a nickname or pet name, even if it isn't. The name you were born with is probably your best byline, but most people have some leeway:

- Deborah Martin
- Deborah A. Martin
- D. A. Martin
- D. Anne Martin

You may think that a byline ought to be striking and memorable, and you may be tempted to invent an elegant nom de plume—Curtis St. John, or something of that sort. I think that would be a mistake. Unless you have some compelling reason to hide your identity, I don't see the point of using a pseudonym. Your byline will take on whatever value you put into it by the quality of your work, whether it is an exotic name like Jerzy Kosinski, or an "ordinary" one like James Jones.

If you are a married woman, bear in mind that you may not always be married to your present spouse; if you take his name now for your byline, you may regret it later.

Work Habits

Good work habits are anything that works for you. Here are some things that have worked for other people.

Have a place to write that is used only by you and only for writing. Set aside certain hours of the day for writing—whatever your circumstances allow, even if it's only two hours on Saturday and Sunday mornings—and use those hours for nothing else. Plan what you are going to write beforehand so that when you go to the keyboard you will be ready to write. In this way you will condition yourself to write whenever you are at the keyboard. If for any reason you find yourself stopped for more than a minute or two, get up, leave the keyboard, sort out your difficulty, and then come back. Keep a notebook handy or carry it with you so that you can jot down thoughts that occur to you at odd moments.

The likelihood is that you will be a part-time writer at least for a number of years and perhaps for your whole writing career. Many distinguished professionals have been part-time writers—have pursued their writing careers while holding down full-time jobs. The most successful of them seem to do it by organizing every available scrap of time: they write on commuter trains, they write in the morning before breakfast, they write whenever they have a few minutes free during the day.

Your life circumstances will be governed by a lot of things not under your control; you may have to work for years at jobs you don't especially like; your marriage may break up; there may be heavy demands on your time and your emotions from children and other members of your family. Ideally you might be spared all this, but if you were, would you have as much to write about? Every experience you live through contributes something to your maturity and your understanding of the world you live in. Even boredom has some value to a writer.

If you have a job that does not completely occupy your mind, you may be able to plan out the day's writing at work, and so be ready to start the moment you sit down at the keyboard. Being a little frustrated about keyboard time may not be a bad thing. Writers who have nothing to do but write often become pencil sharpeners and lint pickers.

A lot of what I tell you in this book is my opinion, and has the weight of authority against it: for instance, Joseph Conrad made himself sit at his desk for a certain number of hours every day, even if he couldn't write a word; John Steinbeck believed that if he couldn't put his theme into one sentence, he wasn't ready to write. I stick to my guns. I think Conrad's self-torment was unnecessary and that he might have accomplished even more if he had trained himself to sit at his desk only when he was writing; and I think Steinbeck's achievement might have been even greater if he had not manipulated his characters to fit his themes (see, for instance, *In Dubious Battle*).

You have the right to know what I think, even if you disagree with it. If you are the sort of writer who believes in training herself by the use of the stick rather than the carrot, or if you really believe you must be able to state your theme before you write, you will do it your way no matter what I tell you (and you should).

Pleasures and Pains

High-school and college teachers of "creative writing" (what other kind is there?) often are too gentle with their students. Their idea is that the students should be encouraged to write, no matter what. In the early stages, writing may be a joy, as long as you don't realize how badly you write. When you find that out, it becomes painful. But students really want to know what's wrong with their writing. Patting them on the head for everything they do is a mistake; it merely frustrates the students, because they sense they are not getting any better.

Learning to write is painful. Learning ballet is painful; learning piano is painful. People willingly undergo this pain and even inflict it on themselves, because they look forward to the joy of mastery.

Somebody once told me, "Show me a person who likes to write and I'll show you a bad writer." Not true. When you have achieved some control and ease, you will find that writing is a joy again.

I bring all this up in order to warn you that in studying technique you may go through a period when you have lost sight of the things that made you want to write in the first place. The joy will be gone, not just because you're doing something hard, but because you have left it out of the mixture. Remember that all the technique in the world won't help you if you have nothing to say. Write the things that are deeply important to you; learn technique to write them better.

Once you are a full-time writer, nobody but you will decide when you start and stop work, get up in the morning or go to bed. Your time will be your own; you can choose your own projects and put in as many hours on them as you please. If you want to take a trip and can afford it, you can go without asking anybody's permission. You can dress any way you like. You won't have to worry about being fired, or about not getting a promotion. You won't even have to *see* anybody you don't like. You will be doing what you like to do and getting paid for it.

That's one side. Now for the other side. It's true that your time will be your own, but unless you use it for something constructive, you won't be able to buy a sandwich or a pair of shoes. When you sell a story, you may wait a year or more to see it in print, and when you do, you may discover that the editor has rewritten it to suit his own conception of style or to fit available space. If you get an agent, she may be the wrong one, and it may take you years to find that out.

If you are living on what you earn from one month to another, without any savings to fall back on, there will be unpleasant periods when you wait every day for the check you have to have, which will certainly not come when you expect it and may never come. You will be tempted over and over to write something inferior for quick cash, and if you are as inept at this as I am, the editor won't buy it. If your income is small and you have a family to support, you will feel guilty for not giving up and taking a job, and if you do take a job, you will feel guilty for giving up your writing.

Frustration and Despair

If you have been writing and submitting stories without success, you already know something about this. Printed rejection slips are not only damaging to your ego, they are uninformative: they don't give you any clue to what you're doing wrong. Even after you begin selling stories, others will be rejected, and you may have no idea why.

What is worse than this is *knowing* what's wrong with your stories, and still not being able to do anything about it. When the thing in your mind is perfectly clear but it doesn't get onto the paper, there may be times when you seriously consider jumping out the window. (I'm glad to say that few writers actually do this.)

At some point in your career, and maybe more than once, you may become convinced that you will never write another line. I know two or three professional writers who say this has never happened to them, but I am not sure they are truthful.

I was blocked on a novel once for over ten years. I finished the novel finally and went on to write other things, but I know the same thing could happen to me again. There is never any assurance that you can write again, no matter how many times you have done it before.

It is cold comfort to say that these are common experiences, that learning a new skill is difficult, and that "learning plateaus," in which you seem to be making no progress at all, are frequent. If you like, think of yourself as a salmon, going up through a series of ladders to spawn; that probably won't help much either.

Remember that I never told you it was easy.

It Isn't a Lottery

You may happen to know that the magazine you're aiming at gets four thousand submissions a year and publishes only forty, and you think your story's chance is one in a hundred, but you're wrong, because it isn't a lottery. If your submission is as bad as 90 percent of them are, your chance of acceptance is not one in a hundred, it is *zero*.

Darrell Schweitzer, a student of mine, pointed this out years ago. If your story shows any sign of life and falls within the magazine's invisible boundaries, its chances of acceptance are much higher than you think—one in twenty, maybe, or even one in four.

Being Publishable

When teachers look at student work, or when editors look at stories in the slushpile, they can always tell roughly how close the author is to being publishable. Here are some of the things they look for:

• A sense of the *transaction* between the author and the reader. Many would-be writers have no such sense; they are not writing for anyone but themselves.

Theodore Sturgeon said he wrote every story as if it were intended to be read by one person, someone he knew. Then he could check to be sure as he went along that he was being clear to that person. Others use "the reader over your shoulder." My reader, when I am writing fiction, is one who shares all my tastes but is a little smarter than I am and knows more than I do. (So I have to be careful not to commit any blunder that will provoke that reader's derision.)

In every professional story there is an implied statement: "I know something you don't know." If you, the writer, *don't* know something we (the readers) don't know, why are you writing?

Well, you say, you're writing to learn how to write. Good, but you can't write about *nothing*. If your head is empty, your story will be too.

• A sense of form. The story should have some perceptible shape, should be rounded and firm, not like a puddle of oatmeal on the floor, or a thread that a cat has been playing with.

• A command of language. You may have wonderful things to express, but you still can't be a writer unless you have some knowledge of syntax (the way words are put together into phrases and sentences) and unless you have a good active vocabulary.

Networking

Earlier in this book I said that I never had any formal instruction in writing, but that is not quite true. In 1943, when I was a very ignorant young writer, I got a job as an assistant editor for Popular Publications, which then had about forty pulp magazines. An assistant editor is a person who does all the donkey work—editing manuscripts, reading proofs, reading slush. By comparing the stories we bought and the ones we rejected, I found out what the difference was without anybody telling me. I realized later that I had had priceless training; I learned more in that office than I could ever have found out in a college writing class.

The reason I got the job was that I was a member of a group of New York fans who called themselves the Futurians; Frederik Pohl, another Futurian who was working for Popular Publications, recommended me. Later I realized that entry-level editorial jobs on fiction magazines were *always* filled that way; they were never advertised, because there were so few openings, and somebody always had a friend who could apply.

I never heard the word "networking" until years later, but that was what it was. ("It isn't what you know but who you know.") Friendless, isolated writers have a much smaller chance of breaking in than those who belong to networks.

Therefore if you are a friendless and isolated writer, seize any opportunity to get into a network. Go to conventions, meet other writers; join workshops if you can; attend writing courses taught by professionals. If you can persuade any known writer to recommend you, your chances of being taken seriously by an editor or agent will shoot up like a rocket.

Slumps

A slump is a drastic slowdown in a writer's production; it may amount to a complete stoppage, in which case it is sometimes referred to as a block. A slump may have any of a number of causes, ranging from simple overwork or illness to psychological problems. It may be a way chosen by the writer's unconscious to tell her that she ought to be writing something different, or it may be nothing but an exacerbation of the writer's normal laziness.

It is my belief that some slumps are benign, but that doesn't make them any easier to live with. I have been through three or four serious slumps, lasting a year or more, and each time have come out the other side writing something quite different and, I think, better. Other writers don't seem to need these drastic reorganization periods, and I certainly don't recommend them.

Writers have worked out various methods of preventing or coping with slumps. In the first category, that of prevention, the habit of working the same hours every day is paramount. Some writers also deliberately stop each day's work at a point when they know what the next sentence is to be, on the theory that that makes it easier to start again the next day. Some read over the unfinished work every day (even if it is a novel); some, having done so, retype the last page or two in order to get back into the rhythm of the story.

Once a slump has occurred, any change in the writer's working habits or circumstances may help to break it—moving to another room, for instance, or writing in longhand, or even adopting a pseudonym. This last method worked for a writer I know who had been blocked for years; as soon as she told herself that the work would not be published under her own name, she could write again.*

Gene Wolfe, the author of *Peace* and *The Fifth Head of Cerberus,* has a system of his own. If he finds himself unable to write, he forbids himself to read anything for recreation, or watch television, or listen to the radio, or go out to any entertainment. Eventually, out of sheer boredom, his unconscious gives in. Under this system, he says, the longest period he has gone without being able to write is four days.

Living with a Writer

Ben Bova, a popular writer and the former editor of *Analog,* says that people who meet writers at conventions and seminars have no idea what they are really like, because they never see writers at

---

*I have never been hung up in that particular way, but I understand it, because in the days before I began using a word processor, I froze if I tried to write on white paper. I used another color (usually blue); that told me that I was typing rough copy and could do whatever I liked.

work. If you marry or live with someone, you ought to give that person some idea of what he or she is in for.

It is very difficult for a nonwriter to understand that writing doesn't take place only at the keyboard; it goes on in the writer's head, sometimes eighteen hours a day or more. There is a story about Renoir that illustrates this. The painter was sitting in his garden one morning when a neighbor passed, raised his hat and said, "Ah, Monsieur Renoir—are you resting?" "No," said Renoir, "working." Later the same neighbor passed and found the painter daubing at a canvas. "Ah, Monsieur Renoir, now you are working?" "No, resting," said Renoir.

When a writer is sitting down, looking at a wall with a blank expression on his face, it is easy for a companion to assume that he isn't doing anything and ought to be available for light conversation, or a discussion of finances, or of the broken washing machine, or whatever.

Even when a writer is actually at the keyboard, it seldom occurs to a nonwriting spouse that he should not be interrupted for any household emergency short of a fire or explosion. Getting ready to write is a complex mental process and a very delicate one; what it feels like to me is that I have laboriously climbed a ladder, carrying my brushes and can of paint. When I am interrupted, it is like being knocked off the ladder. Two or three such interruptions can be so discouraging that I no longer want to climb the ladder.

Once at the Milford Conference we asked all the writers to talk about their minimum requirements for work. The responses were varied, but one thing everybody agreed on: They needed a certain amount of free time ahead of them—time without distractions or interruptions. If I know I haven't got that free time, the writing process doesn't even start.

Other people go to work in the morning and come home at night; a writer is always in the house. That may be hard for a spouse to take, if she is at home all day too. "How do you stand having him around all the time?" a woman once asked my wife. I don't think she meant anything special about me; she was just thinking how awful it would be if her own husband didn't go to work and leave her alone.

Another problem for spouses, and children too, is that most people think of writing as a sort of hobby rather than an occupation. (When he was small, my youngest son asked his mother why I didn't have a truck like all the other kids' fathers.)

These are some of the reasons why I think I am lucky to have been married to another writer for many years. Another is that we have never run out of things to talk about. Isolation is the price most writers pay for their freedom, and it is a heavy one. Other writers have to travel hundreds of miles, at great expense, to find anybody to talk to about what interests them most; we just have to sit down at the kitchen table.

If you have not yet decided whether you really want to be a professional writer, it may be a little premature to discuss how to meet other writers in order to marry one. I wouldn't suggest going to writing classes or workshops for this purpose, but it often does work out that way. My wife and I met at the Milford Conference, which I was running at that time in Milford, Pennsylvania. A number of our students at the Clarion Workshop at Michigan State University have paired off and married. If you get a job in publishing you will be exposed to writers and also to editors, who are a similar breed.

Ideally, perhaps, a writer would marry an older person who is benevolent, permissive, and very rich, but I don't know how to tell you to go about that.

Typewriters and Other Keyboards

Here and there in this book when I talk about your writing, I say "when you are at the keyboard," but you may not want to work that way at all. Richard McKenna, the author of *The Sand Pebbles,* wrote his first drafts in longhand with a mechanical pencil—it had to be the same mechanical pencil—and revised on the typewriter. I know another writer who worked in pen for most of his career, using different colors of ink; when he got tired of one, he switched to another.

People got along without typewriters and other keyboards for thousands of years, and some of them wrote more in their lifetimes than I ever expect to. There are two problems involved in writing by hand: one is writer's cramp, a painful and disabling spasm of the fingers, and the other is illegibility. Kate Wilhelm began writing in longhand, but she discovered after a while that when she retyped she was really doing the story over, because she couldn't read her own writing. She taught herself to compose on the typewriter, but it was six months before the machine stopped getting in her way.

In the first edition of this book I had some disparaging things to say about word processors. That was before I got one.

I worked for twenty years on a manual Royal typewriter, a marvelously reliable machine; in all that time, it never needed any repairs, and it was still functioning when I gave it away in 1962. Then I went to a series of electric typewriters, beginning with a second-hand IBM Model A, another marvelous machine, so beautifully designed that when anything went wrong with it, I could usually fix it myself.

The last of my electric typewriters was falling apart when my son Christopher bought a computer and coaxed me into trying it. In the next eight months I turned out as many pages as I had done in the previous two years.

To my surprise, all the things I had heard about word processing turned out to be true. The machine takes care of nearly all the drudgery of writing—editing, transposing text, retyping. It reduces fatigue, and it does away with the fear of making mistakes, because they are so easy to correct.

There are spelling programs now, a necessity for some writers comparable to insulin, and even programs that will correct your syntax. The next thing, I am told, will be the elimination of the keyboard itself—computers will be voice-actuated. But I suspect that some writers will cling to their typewriters, and even to their mechanical pencils.

Drugs and Writing

The only book on writing that I ever read when I was young was Jack Woodford's *Trial and Error*. Most of the advice in it was useless to me, but Woodford said one thing that I took to heart and have profited by ever since. He said, in effect, Don't drink when you're writing. In the first place, alcohol is a central nervous system depressant that makes you dumber, not smarter, and in the second place, if you get in the habit of writing when you drink, you may find yourself unable to write unless you are drinking.

My experience with other drugs is limited to two or three experiments with marijuana, which I didn't much like, so I will not pose as an expert, but I suspect that what is true of alcohol is true of most of them. A friend of mine ingested some morning-glory seeds in the 1960s, when they were popular, and he told me that a few hours later he found himself staring at two oddly shaped leather objects on the floor. He struggled with their significance and finally broke through into a dazzling revelation, viz.: *"Feet* go into *shoes!"* It was his opinion that psychedelic drugs, rather than expanding your consciousness, contract it so much that the most banal thought seems brilliant.

Writing itself, on the other hand, *does* expand your consciousness, and it is almost the only thing I know that does.

Reference Books

If you are living in apartments and moving frequently, you may have to travel light. Once you get settled, you ought to buy reference books, beginning with the best dictionary you can afford. Mine is the Merriam-Webster Unabridged, Third Edition. Anybody can call a dictionary "Webster's" (after Noah Webster, the author of the first American dictionary), but the Merriam-Webster is the standard reference dictionary and the final authority in this country. I also have a two-volume set of the *Oxford English Dictionary,* which I got as a premium when I joined a book club; the type is so small that it has to be read with a magnifying glass. I use it maybe five or six times a year, when I can't find something in Webster. And I have a long shelf of foreign-language dictionaries; I use the Latin, German, French, and Spanish fairly frequently, but there are others I never have used and probably never will, unless I take up the study of Finnish or Albanian.

If you own a good dictionary and use it only to look up spellings, you are not getting your money's worth. Whenever you look up a word for any reason, read the definitions (all of them), and read the *derivations*. Words are not just signs, they are clusters of meaning and association.

The *Harbrace College Handbook* is an excellent guide to syntax, usage, etc. Mine is the 7th, which has exercises that were dropped from later editions.

If you are interested in your own language, you will find *The Story of English,* by Mario Pei, a fascinating introductory work. *The American Language,* by H. L. Mencken, is a delight to read. So are *Modern English Usage,* by H. W. Fowler, and *The King's English,* by Fowler and his brother, even though they are about a century out of date.

I don't own a thesaurus and am prejudiced against them, but you may feel differently about that. I have Bartlett's *Familiar Quotations* and *The Oxford Dictionary of Quotations,* and several others that are fun to read but not much good for reference. I have three copies of the King James Bible, all inherited; one would be enough. I seem to have mislaid my French Bible, which I got because I read about it in Clarence Day's *Life with Father:* where the King James says, "Blessed are the meek," the French says, "Happy are the debonnaire."

I have a 1965 set of the *Encyclopaedia Britannica,* and I use it often. The *Britannica* is available on-line now, at a price that I think is steep. New print encyclopedias are expensive, too, but used sets can be found in large secondhand book stores, and they are bargains.

A good atlas is next; I have the one that came with the encyclopedia, and several other large ones. I also keep any maps that fall into my hands; road maps are particularly useful. (If my character is driving from San Francisco to Laramie, for instance, I need to know what towns she will pass through on the way, etc.)

I have a lot of science books that I got for nothing when I was a book reviewer, but I seldom use any of them for reference. I sometimes refer to Isaac Asimov's *The Intelligent Man's Guide to Science.* Even more useful, however, are two high-school textbooks, one on physics, the other on chemistry, that I got from one of the kids in the family.

A current almanac is a very useful thing, and if I had been bright enough I would have kept all my old ones. If you are writing about 1958, say, you need to know what people knew *then,* not what they know now. I have a recent edition of the *Merck Manual,* a physicians' handbook, and refer to it often. I also have a copy of the 1940 edition; the contrast between the two is instructive.

For "style" in the copy editor's sense—things like punctuation, division of words, use of italics, and so on—the authority is *The Chicago Manual of Style,* published by the University of Chicago Press.

Your interests and needs for reference works are certain to be different from mine, and you should follow your instincts. About twenty years ago I began to feel an irresistible urge to buy any anthology of general fiction that I saw in a used-book store. There was no apparent reason for that, but much later, when I realized that I wanted to write this book, those anthologies were on my shelf and I used them. If you ever feel a sudden passion for books about the lives of the saints, or Oriental carpets, or marine biology, Fred is probably trying to tell you something. Give in.

There are some other reference works that you probably will not want to buy, but you ought to be aware that they are available at public libraries. One is *The Readers' Guide to Periodical Literature,* which indexes magazine articles by title, author, and subject. Another is *The Short Story Index;* it lists short fiction by title and author. There are other specialized indexes that you may want to consult from time to time. Reference librarians are highly skilled and resourceful people; if what you want is available, they will show you where to find it.

Incidentally, if your local library doesn't have a book, they will order it for you through the interlibrary loan service. Brand-new books are usually not available this way, but if the one you want is a year or more old, you will probably get it. If the book you want is a new one, you can put in a purchase request, and very often the library will buy it. When it comes they will let you know, and you will be the first borrower.

What Should You Read?

Everything. You should read Shakespeare and William Gibson and Dostoevsky, and you should read the labels on ketchup bottles, but you should read everything when you want to read it. If you approach any reading as drudgery, it will be drudgery. Try the classics from time to time, but if you find them boring or incomprehensible, put them down again. You may not be ready yet. (Remember the thrifty New Englander who always made his family eat the bad apples first. By the time they had eaten the bad ones, more good ones had turned bad, and so on, until they got to the bottom of the barrel without ever having eaten a good apple.) There are some books esteemed by others that never will have anything to say to you, and there are books you will love all alone, and that's the way it should be. Read books that excite you, whether they're about flying saucers or Jungian psychology or deep-sea fishing. They will keep the blood flowing in your brain, and sooner or later all this information will bob to the surface in your fiction.

Moving Up

Throughout this book, in many ways, I have been trying to caution you against doing imitative work. I want to summarize these admonitions here. If you copy anyone else, you will inevitably lose some of the vitality and strength of the original. If, in the effort to conform to the requirements of a commercial market, you pay them lip service, your work will be insincere and unconvincing. Worse, you will have left out the only thing you really have to offer, your own talent, your own personality and convictions. Even if you succeed in being published, you will find yourself among the unremembered writers, those who are bought only as a last resort.

The only way to real success in writing is to find some space, even if it is only a small corner, that only you can fill. Once you have done this and have begun to be published with some regularity, opportunities will come along; you may be offered a job or two. Magazines will begin printing your name on their covers; editors will ask, "When are you going to send me another story?"

Eventually, perhaps before you are old and gray, your stories will be reprinted in anthologies. You will be invited to lecture or to conduct writing workshops. Younger writers will seek your company, hoping for words of wisdom.

Do not write me complaining letters if none of this happens to you. There is no law that says it has to, but if you write honestly and with dedication, you will probably find that virtue really is rewarded; it just takes a while.

SUGGESTED READING

Most of these books are out of print, but they are well worth hunting up in libraries and used-book stores.

Tellers of Tales, edited by W. Somerset Maugham (Doubleday, 1940). This giant anthology contains a hundred short stories from Europe and the United States. Maugham's introduction, which is twenty-seven pages long, is superb. If you have only one historical anthology of short fiction, this should be the one. (I can't imagine why you would ever need another.)

Short Stories, edited by Sean O'Faolain (Little, Brown, 1961). I like this anthology because the stories are good, and because O'Faolain's comments are cheerful and perceptive. He discusses the stories according to the various kinds of pleasure they give the reader, and that's not a bad idea, although it is hopeless to restrict the number of these kinds of pleasure to eight. Each story is followed by a series of academic questions, but you can skip them.

Those Who Can, edited by Robin Scott Wilson (New American Library, 1973). Twelve stories, each with an essay by the author, grouped under six headings: plot, character, setting, theme, point of view, and style. Some of the authors and their topics are mismatched, but several of the essays are strikingly original and good. The book also contains my annotated "Masks."

Paragons, edited by Robin Scott Wilson (St. Martin's, 1996). Twenty-four stories and essays by a newer group of authors.

The Creative Process, edited by Brewster Ghiselin (University of California Press, 1952; New American Library, 1955). This is an eye-opening book: thirty-nine sections in which writers, poets, artists, mathematicians, musicians, dancers, philosophers, and scientists tell how they work. Einstein, for instance, said that he thought, not in words or mathematical symbols, but in kinesthetic sensations.

"Journey with a Little Man." This essay by Richard McKenna can be found in the following books: *The Sons of Martha and Other Stories,* by Richard McKenna (Harper & Row, 1964); *Chapel Hill Carousel,* edited by Jessie Rehder (University of North Carolina Press, 1967); *New Eyes for Old,* by Richard McKenna (John F. Blair, 1972); *Turning Points,* edited by Damon Knight (Harper & Row, 1977).

Storytellers and Their Art, edited by Georgianna Trask and Charles Burkhart (Doubleday, 1963). Brief excerpts from writings by and about famous authors, arranged under five headings. The selections are lively, and the cheek-by-jowl arrangement makes them even livelier. (Under the subheading "Talent," for instance, you will find Hemingway, Tolstoy, and Thomas Mann, all on one page.) If you are fascinated by what writers have to say about their own work, you will love this book.

Plotting and Writing Suspense Fiction, by Patricia Highsmith (The Writer, 1966). Sensible, good-humored, and practical advice from a distinguished mystery writer. Much of what she says about novels can be applied to short stories.

INDEX

201

ABOUT THE AUTHOR

Damon Knight has written over eighty short stories, fourteen novels, and three nonfiction books, and he has edited numerous anthologies and magazines, but he is probably best known as a master of short fiction. His many writing awards include the Jupiter Award for best short story, the Pilgrim Award for his general contribution to science fiction, the C. E. S. Wood Award for contributions to Oregon letters, and the Hugo Award for best science-fiction criticism. He is cofounder and former director of the Milford (Pennsylvania) Science Fiction Writers' Conference, a former lecturer at the Clarion Writers' Workshop at Michigan State University, and the founder and first president of Science Fiction Writers of America. He lives with his wife, Kate Wilhelm, in Eugene, Oregon.